70103953

It is with great anticipation that I have waited for the revealing of this book. I have devoured it as a revelation from God. In a world that has almost dismissed any kind of structure in the kingdom of God, this book stands as a reminder that God builds with intention and accuracy. God is the God of forethought, planning and the execution of those plans! It is as though you can almost feel His hands as He systematically forms the structure of the human body down to the smallest part from the dust of the earth. I am blessed by the revelation that is held inside the pages of this book. Every great painter signs his completed work and it is no mystery that the God of the eternal ages would do the same! What is shocking is the detail in which it is signed. Every piece so intricately made with the stamp of the creator, every piece shouting out a witness to the divine hand of God. Terry Swiger will take you on a journey through the temple that God has blessed you with and at every corner she will bring you face to face with the signature of the God who created you! My prayer is that God will use this book to bring unbelievers into the realm of faith in God as they see His handy work that is right under our noses!

—Pastor Robert Clegg

Walk through the Temple of Your Own Body

Discover Hidden Secrets of God's Image

Terry Swiger

WESTBOW®
PRESS
A DIVISION OF THOMAS NELSON
& ZONDERVAN

Copyright © 2014 Terry Jane Swiger.

All rights reserved. No part of this book may be used or reproduced by any means, graphic, electronic, or mechanical, including photocopying, recording, taping or by any information storage retrieval system without the written permission of the publisher except in the case of brief quotations embodied in critical articles and reviews.

WestBow Press books may be ordered through booksellers or by contacting:

WestBow Press
A Division of Thomas Nelson & Zondervan
1663 Liberty Drive
Bloomington, IN 47403
www.westbowpress.com
1 (866) 928-1240

Because of the dynamic nature of the Internet, any web addresses or links contained in this book may have changed since publication and may no longer be valid. The views expressed in this work are solely those of the author and do not necessarily reflect the views of the publisher, and the publisher hereby disclaims any responsibility for them.

Any people depicted in stock imagery provided by Thinkstock are models, and such images are being used for illustrative purposes only. Certain stock imagery © Thinkstock.

ISBN: 978-1-4908-2583-0 (sc)
ISBN: 978-1-4908-2582-3 (hc)
ISBN: 978-1-4908-2584-7 (e)

Library of Congress Control Number: 2014902321

Printed in the United States of America.

WestBow Press rev. date: 03/10/2014

Contents

Purpose

Discover Hidden Secrets of God's Image

As you walk through the temple of your own body; you will discover hidden secrets of God's image designed throughout your bone structure. You will also experience *just how* fearfully and wonderfully made you really are!

God said, "Let Us make man in Our image, according to Our likeness, So God created man in His own image; in the image of God He created him; male and female He created them. (Genesis 1:26-27) NKJ

I believe Our Heavenly Father has given us this gift of encouragement; that we will allow His power to flow through us more freely.

And what agreement has the temple of God with idols? For you are the temple of the living God. As God has said, "I will dwell in them, and walk among them. I will be their God, and they shall be my people." (II Corinthians 6:16)

Dedication

First and foremost, I dedicate this book to bring Glory and Honor to my Heavenly Father and Jesus Christ as Lord. To my husband Darrell for his love and encouragement to complete what the Lord had laid upon my heart. To our two daughters and their families who have given me there unwavering support: And a special dedication to all our grandchildren.

Preface and Introduction

This amazing journey through the temple of our body started with a simple human anatomy lesson. The study of the human anatomy was a vital part of a two-year program in order to begin my home-based business.

The first part of the program was a welcomed challenge for this accomplished homemaker; but something about the musculoskeletal system part of my human anatomy lesson caused me to be more than just a little anxious. I can still recall how cold chills traveled up and down my spine as I flipped through the pages where the diagrams of our skeletal bones were systematically illustrated. It seemed as if the very bones in the pictures actually rose up from off the pages to greet me and then to taunt me at the same time. Before I knew it, something inside me had awakened into a full rebellion that threw me into what I will describe as a frozen state of panic! Now as a rational person I knew that the whole eerie episode was certainly uncalled for and it didn't take long for me to take the grueling matter to God in prayer.

When I prayed, I sensed God's loving presence in the most peaceful fashion, at the same time was made aware that what I had experienced was a spirit of fear. This presence of God's Holy Spirit brought calmness around me like a warm blanket of comfort to where I had truly come to know the peace that passes all understanding. Within those same precious moments, it was made clear to me that the Holy Spirit was going to walk me through the human bone structure. From that moment on, that spirit of fear had vanished.

During our walk through the skeletal structure, this amazing Teacher graciously unveiled many hidden secrets of God's image with the upmost intimacy. Because of the Holy Spirit's insight and guidance His light had shown into all the reference materials that I had on hand. Certain words and numerical values were as golden nuggets highlighted along our path of study, and each one was expounded upon as being founded upon God's word.

Those same golden nuggets led up to reveal God's hidden images. God's very own clever handiwork was discovered as if from a carpenter's blueprint within my own body as well as every man, woman and child. Our Heavenly Father's very own patterned designs of His images have been locked securely within man since He made Adam. And Oh yes they exceed far above all the animals that God Created.

I was introduced to God's images that include designed patterns to be symbolic of Jesus' birth, life and ministry, the crucifixion and the fruits/ gifts of the Holy Spirit. Revelation 4:2-4 has a powerful God image of its own that is truly incredible. Each and every Image of God relates to Genesis 1:26. I was constantly reminded that these images of God, and more, were first framed within Adam's own bone structure.

God said, **"Let Us make man in Our image, according to Our likeness**, So **God created man in His own image**; in the image of God He created him (Adam); male and female He created them. (Genesis 1:26-27) "(emphasis added)."

And what agreement has the temple of God with idols? **For you are the temple** of the living God. As God has said**: "I will dwell in them, and walk among them.** I will be their God, and they shall be my people." (II Corinthians 6:16) "(emphasis added)."

By the conclusion of our first walk together I was left with yet another great surprise! The bonus was that of the bony appearance of a smile on our human skull. On the very top of this totally fresh revelation is an image of God that portrays a pleasant smile of satisfaction; A joyful countenance that wants to encourage confidence in our Heavenly Father's Love for all people.

The direct opposite of how it has been portrayed in the secular world by some; only because of misunderstanding, of course.

God loves all people, and I believe that He wants to share His hidden secrets with his people. It is written in Deuteronomy 29:29, **The secret things belong unto the Lord our God: But those things are which revealed belong to us and to our children forever, that we may do all the words of this law**. "(emphasis added)."

In conclusion I must add, from time to time I have been reminded of Jeremiah, known as the weeping prophet. God illustrated something important to me though Jeremiah as he watched the potter working at the wheel. He watched as the skillful potter would stop the wheel from spinning then crushed the clay that he was working with.

When Jeremiah asked why, the potter remarked that there was a flaw in the clay. God helped Jeremiah realize that there is a flaw in His people. Our flaw is in our covenant relationship with our Heavenly Father and it reflects in our very nature. It is the flaw that causes us to flow against God rather than to just go with God. That is a fatal flaw! I believe the Holy Spirit has given us this fresh vision of God's image designed within our body as encouragement to correct that flaw!

God has a perfect plan for me and you, and that is to be made into the perfect likeness of His Son Jesus Christ. When we turn ourselves over to God by faith knowing Him be our Potter and Designer, He will ultimately walk each one of us into His magnificent purpose… just the way He made us to be.

I have done my best although probably not so perfectly worded, to share this precious gift of why God loves all people everywhere. I have no reason to believe that it came by none other than the Holy Spirit of our Heavenly Father, Jesus.

Terry Jane Swiger, January 2014

Part 1

The Temple
Overview and Background

And what agreement has the temple of God with idols? For you are the temple of the living God. As God has said, "I will dwell in them, and walk among them. I will be their God, and they shall be my people." (II Corinthians 6:16) New King James

Chapter 1

The Temple

In the New Testament, in Acts 17:22–24, Paul stood in the midst of Areopagus and said, "Men of Athens, I perceive that in all things you are very religious; for as I was passing through and considering the objects of your worship, I even found an altar with this inscription: TO THE UNKNOWN GOD. Therefore, the One whom you worship without knowing, Him I proclaim to you: "God, who made the world and everything in it, since He is Lord of heaven and earth, does not dwell in temples made with hands."

Paul also reinforced that each individual's body was a temple designed for the Holy Spirit. In 1 Corinthians 3:16–17 Paul pleads with the Corinthian believers to rebuild their broken relationships with God: "Do you not know that you are the temple of God and that the Spirit of God dwells in you? If anyone defiles the temple of God, God will destroy him. For the temple of God is holy, which temple you are.

The apostle Paul not only reminds us what our body is, but also of its intended purpose.

By the end of our walk together through our skeletal system, there will be a clearer understanding as to why 1 Corinthians 3:17 carries the warning with it. Paul said that if anyone defiles God's temple, God will destroy him or her. What a sobering statement!

As we travel through our skeletal foundation, God, through His Holy Spirit will reveal His images within our temple's foundation.

God's Images have been locked securely in place within our bones from the days of creation when God made Adam and Eve.

This walk will also reveal visual proof that people have not evolved from any fish, animal, or thing that God has given us dominion over according to Genesis 1:27–28!

So God created man in His own image, and in the image of God He created him; male and female He created them. Then God blessed them, and God said to them, "Be fruitful, and multiply; fill the earth, and subdue it; have dominion over the fish of the sea, over the birds of the air, and over everything that moves on the earth. Genesis 1:27–28 confirms man's rightful authority over this earth, but not apart from God's indwelling presence.

A Battle Rages against the Temple

From the beginning of our existence described in Genesis in Chapter 1:26 Then God said, "**Let Us make man in Our image** according to **Our likeness**; let them have dominion over the fish of the sea, over the birds of the air..." (emphasis added); God created within man a HUNGER FOR HIS PRESENCE. Satan brought on his sinister side whose "ego" demands that he be God.

Satan has always known that people were designed to mirror God's image from the very beginning, so it's no wonder that he has spread his disease of hate and jealousy through wars of destruction, brother against brother, nation against nation, and kingdom against kingdom. By the end of this walk through the temple, one will realize why the enemy comes to steal, kill, and destroy us. The only attraction that Satan's demon spirits have to God's image is to use it while he abuses it. When bad things happen to good people, the same questions are asked over and over, "Why is this happening to me, what did I do wrong?" The information given by the Holy Spirit will answer this very question.

But John 3:16 still holds strong, **For God so loved the world that He gave His only begotten Son, that whoever believes in him shall not perish but have everlasting life. "**(emphasis added)."

You are from God, little children, and have overcome them, because **He who is in you is greater than he who is in the world!** (I John 4:4) "(emphasis added)."

All people, especially the born again believer needs to be able to stand confident not only for themselves, but as an encouragement for others during these last days. This perfect design of God has always been under attack by Satan and demonic forces. These forces have their own evil desires and agendas to dishonor the temple and to destroy it.

Today, Satan has accelerated competition while using the anti-Christ's of this world to do everything possible to intellectually distort and camouflage God's spiritual image within man. Satan has succeeded by brainwashing people to believe that they can become strong by adopting the images of this secular world in which we live. This falsehood has instilled insecurity within countless people as they have become dependent upon the kingdom of this world rather than the kingdom of God.

In John 10:10 Jesus reminds us that the thief walks alongside every man, woman, and child, (especially the unprotected unborn) to steal, kill and destroy.

But the good news is that Jesus says, "I have come that they may have life, and that they may have it more **abundantly**.

We have to remember that the Enemy (Satan) has always had insight into this Scripture: **As you do not know what is the way of the wind,** *or how the bones grow in the womb of her that is with child,* **so you do not know the works of God who makes everything.** (Ecclesiastes 11:5) (emphasis added).

5

Today, your eyes will be enlightened of the hidden secrets of how the bones are placed together in the womb! The mighty works of our God!

By the time this walk through the temple is complete, you will fully understand "why" the Enemy continually pursues people with his mission to steal, kill, and destroy. The Devil knows that he can enter the temple of our physical bodies by the door of our own ignorance (most of the time by our own naïve invitations) with his deceitful plan to destroy the temple from the inside out through doubt, spiritual blindness, corruption, and physical disease.

Be a Defender of the Temple

All people have the potential to be the greatest warrior when it comes to defending their temple, as they put on the full armor of God described in Ephesians 6:13: "Therefore take up the whole armor of God, that you may be able to **withstand** in the evil day, and having done all, to stand."

Ephesians 6:14–18 refers to Having your loins girt about with truth and having on the breastplate of righteousness; and your feet shod with the preparation of the gospel of peace; Above all taking the shield of faith, in which we will be able to withstand the fiery darts of the wicked, (on a daily basis). The reality of the helmet of salvation was purchased by Jesus. The sword of the Spirit, is demonstrated by speaking the word of God; Praying always with all prayer and supplication in the Spirit.

"Spirit- filled temples," fully dressed in the armor of God, are not only to protect their own temples, but also have been given prayer power for their loved ones too.

The outcome of what the Holy Spirit has revealed is also for an awakening of dry bones spoken of in Ezekiel 37:4 for the whole house of Israel: **A gift wrapped message sealed with His devotion of**

love for the Bride of Christ for an unshakeable confidence as the whole armor of God is worn.

These hidden secrets of God's image support 1 John 4:4, which says, **"You are from God, little children, and have overcome them, because He who is in you is greater than he who is in the world."** (emphasis added).

For example, in the book of Matthew 4, we read that Jesus was led by the Holy Spirit into the wilderness for forty days and nights *to be* tempted by the Devil.

But Jesus was victorious over all three temptations by confidently quoting the Word of God. Jesus spoke the Word with confidence and authority because **Jesus knew what He was and who He was!**

Jesus said: "Believe Me that I am in the Father and the Father in Me, or else believe Me for the sake of the works themselves. **Most assuredly, I say to you, he who believes in Me, the works that I do he will do also; and greater works than these he will do, because I go to My Father.** And whatever you ask in my name, that will I do, that the Father may be glorified in the Son. If you ask anything in my name I will do it." (John14:11–14) (emphasis added).

As we read throughout the New Testament, we find out that the very demons that spoke to Jesus knew that **Jesus knew who He was**, and **with confidence in His authority**, Jesus went about **doing the will of His Father**.

We must transform our minds to how we are *fearfully and wonderfully made*. We need to become confident in God's Word, speak it, and stand on all of God's promises!

There is something the late Oral Roberts said that has always stuck with me, He said, **"Faith is when you know that you know deep within your knower."**

I believe as one walks through the temple of their own body, an important key of wisdom and understanding will be found to unlock a more unshakeable faith to stand firm during these last days. Your own bones will come alive to a greater sense of purpose and power to live as God's temple like never before!

After one walks through the temple of their own body it would be good to go back and read over the question God asked Ezekiel in chapter 37. God took Ezekiel down to the valley that was full of dry bones where the Lord asked Ezekiel if those bones could ever live again. God instructed Ezekiel to prophesy over the dry bones that they would hear the word of the Lord! When he did, there was a shaking as the dry bones came together, bone to his bone. Then muscle tissue, flesh and skin covered the bones. Finally, the Lord caused breath to enter them so they would live; then they stood upon their feet in an exceeding great army.

The Lord told Ezekiel that those bones were the whole house of Israel scattered among the heathen. In Ezekiel chapter 37, it says that previously the bones actually spoke and said that their hope was lost because they had lost their way. The Lord ultimately restored them, healed them and put His spirit in them.

My prayer is that all believers in Jesus Christ as Lord, will be personally edified, restored and encouraged to not lose hope because Jesus said in John 14 verse 6, "I am the way, the truth and the life..."

Chapter 2

Fearfully and Wonderfully Made

In Psalm 139:13-15 David wrote, **"For you formed my inward parts**: You covered me in my mother's womb. I will praise You, for **I am fearfully and wonderfully made**; marvelous are Your works, and that my soul knows very well. **My frame was not hidden from You, when I was made in secret**, and skillfully wrought in the lowest parts of the earth..." NKJ "(emphasis added)."

God knew that David loved him with all his heart, and because of that love, a spiritual revelation of praise blossomed within David that even he himself could not fully explain. David's soul may not have known the specific details of God's handiwork, but to the best of David's understanding he expressed it in Psalms 139.

Today, because of the Holy Spirit's recent tutoring throughout the human skeletal structure, anyone will be able to walk through their own temple's foundation and experience God's marvelous works. Like David, we too can choose to sing a song of praise as the images of God begin to bud, then gloriously bloom like a flower showing off God's skillful handiwork. I am confident that our Creator's clever images designed of Himself will be seen to captivate ones interest as we take a close inspection of our temples foundation.

I found it interesting too to what, Solomon, David's son wrote in Ecclesiastes *11:5*: As you do not know what is the way of the wind, or how the bones grow in the womb of her who is with child, so you do not know the works of God who makes everything.

In the Hebrew text, the word *fearfully* means with *great reverence* and with *heartfelt respect*. The word *wonderfully* that is also used in Psalms 139:13-19 means...unique, set apart, and uniquely marvelous.

As the Holy Spirit walks us through the temple of our body, one will walk away from this personal journey with a brand new confidence that all people, red, yellow, black and white are definitely unique and set apart from every other created beast, great and small. And on the personal level, hope through our Maker's Love, will arise with each enlightening step as we examine the bones of our skeletal structures.

By our journeys end, the Holy Spirit will have revealed God's images as a divine mystery held by the smile on our bony skull's face. The timeline of Jesus' life and ministry will be seen to have been cleverly patterned into our bone structure along with symbolic bone designs of His birth and crucifixion. Revelations 4:2-4 has been designed within the human skeletal structure in a place not to be found in any other created animal that God made from the time of creation.

The symbolic bone placement of the Sword of the Spirit will be found to be represented within God's image and so will the symbolic pattern for His gifts of the Holy Spirit. There is so much more to be discovered as one takes the eye opening adventure through God's temple wonderfully designed for Him to live, breath and walk in.

The outcome of this walk through the temple should cause one to be encouraged to freely welcome God's presence through this Holy Spirit to move in with his permanent residence of strength and everlasting peace. The Holy Spirit longs to fill his people with God's Love, acceptance and peace to replace all the modern day discouragements that we all have faced! Not to forget the uncertainty that this world's economic future holds. We cannot keep our eyes fixed on those things they have a way of bringing on anxiety and anger. **Anxiety and anger are keys that the enemy uses within ones temple to open the door for most all diseases**!

In Ephesians 2:10 it is written, For we are His **workmanship**, created in Jesus Christ for good works, which God prepared beforehand that we should walk in them." (emphasis added).

The word, *Workmanship,* in the Greek means….a work of art brought forth by an artisan; our creator and Heavenly Father.

I am most confident that our **Heavenly Father's visual workmanship** that has been revealed will put the final touches on the **"missing link to being His divine creation."**

Seeing is Believing

The simple fact is seeing believes, even though it would be greater if people would just merely believe without seeing, but consider what Jesus did for Thomas! Maybe, just maybe, this insight is for all the doubting Thomas's that want to believe, but want to see and feel something tangible as evidence. Jesus certainly did not leave Thomas behind before He ascended into heaven. Jesus heard his hearts' cry to believe that Jesus really did come to life again and Jesus did not disappoint him. Jesus gave him something special, something he could visually see and touch as a secure anchor to believe upon.

And after eight days His disciples were again inside, and Thomas with them. Jesus came, the doors being shut, stood in the midst, and said, "Peace to you!" Then He said to Thomas," Reach your finger here, and look at My hands, and reach your hand here, and put it into My side. Do not be unbelieving, but believing. And Thomas answered and said to Him," My Lord and my God." Jesus said to him, "Thomas, because you have seen Me, you believed, Blessed are those who have not seen and yet have believed." (John 20:26-29)

Jesus did not leave Thomas behind without showing him something to believe in visually. And just as Jesus loved Thomas, he most certainly will not forget the ones in these last days who need to see to believe. God's love is for all people and He wants all of us to walk throughout our lives with conviction, confidence, and love for the people around us. After all, Jesus gave two great commandments; love God with all your heart, mind, and soul, and love your neighbor as yourself; all because we are fearfully and wonderfully made!

Chapter 3

Overview of My first Walk through the Temple

This amazing walk through the temple of our body happened as the result of taking a home study course on medical transcription. I can still remember how excited I was to take the course; and then when finished, I could set up my own home based business typing doctor's reports.

As an eager student, I went to work on my new homebound project. It didn't take long for me to complete the medical terminology part of the course. And then I worked my way through the integumentary system concerning the connective tissues, skin, hair, etc. At first the human anatomy did not seem like it was going to be too big a problem for me. Well at least, not until I had turned to the pages that revealed the different diagrams of the musculoskeletal system. As silly as it might sound to some, the craziest sensation of panic whaled up from within me; to the point that the human muscular and bone structure had become absolutely repulsive. As an adult, it wasn't hard for me to recognize that there was something strangely unnatural going on to cause such a fuss over the human skeletal structure.

The musculoskeletal system should have been simple to study: After all, every person who is alive has one and in fact, those who ever lived had one. Within every human body, hidden beneath all the skin tissue is the musculoskeletal system that is the very "backbone" of the human body! This structure makes it possible for people to stand upright as well as supports the soft tissues within our body. Realistically, I shouldn't have had any abnormal reactions to the study, but I quickly picked upon the fact that what I had come against was a definite spirit of fear!

Evidently, that spirit had lain quietly within me for years, and then all of a sudden rose up ever so quickly to strike out in a rage as to fight for its place of residency. Its rebellious nature caused me not want to study anything more about the human bone structure. I even contemplated resigning from the program.

I knew deep down in my soul that I would not be able get passed the emotional roadblock of fear by my own strength. All that turmoil brought against my mind caused me to wonder why the spirit of fear was even in me in the first place. After all, I am a grown adult and had thought that on the spiritual level I had overcome any childish hindrances of the past. As I gave it more thought, I found comfort in the realization that God knew about the tormenting fear within me all along. God knew that one day I would have to recognize the fear and would call upon His help to deal with it!

I believe God helped me to look back over my early childhood years to remind me that it really never did take much for me to get discouraged over the simplest of challenges. During those times, I couldn't even put my finger on any reasons as to why.

My mother told me later that she had an episode of a scare when she was about eight months pregnant for me! It happened late one night when my father was not at home, as he had often worked the afternoon shift. She recalled when she saw an unknown man's face peering at her through the window of the front door of our home. She then went on to tell me how she was instantly gripped with fear. Now, according to "old wives' tales" she told me how such instances could mark a mother's baby. To this day, she still believes those tales handed down to her from her peers. Mother told me that I must have been marked at that time in her pregnancy regardless of her attempt to control her emotions. She recalled that during my early infant and toddler development, about the countless times that I would scream when my father or any man would come near me. But, my father was a loving and companionate man, and because of his persistence we grew into a healthy loving relationship. My father and I were best of friends. He is with the Lord now. Sometimes I wonder if he had a hand in getting me this information for this manuscript! I will certainly ask him when I see him again.

As I reflect back now to the hour when I had reluctantly turned the pages of the anatomy textbook to look over some the different bone structures, the very images threw me into what I have already described as horrific and I knew that I had to stop and go immediately into prayer about it! God had never failed me in the past and He had always been faithful about answering my prayers during my most trying times. As I asked Him for His help this time, His answer came *in a way* different than I could have ever expected. His response was not only instant, but a surprise to me as to the *way* He answered my prayer. It was if God had kept a watchful eye on me during my whole dilemma and was just biding His time for His chance to become my rescuer. At the very moment I asked for His help, a great calmness swept over me likened to a warm blanket of peace. Along with peace, the Spirit of the Lord quickly took over the reigns of my mind and broke through the tormenting roadblock of emotions; needless to say, "that spirit that had tormented me vanished!" Then, I was given the vivid understanding that the Holy Spirit would be my very own personal Tutor throughout the human skeletal structure! God's supernatural presence did indeed become my Teacher through the duration of the study.

Part 2

Made in God's Image

Then God said, "Let Us make **man** in Our image, according to Our likeness; let them have dominion over the fish of the sea, over the birds of the air, and over the cattle, over all the earth and over every creeping thing that creeps on the earth."

So God created man in His *own* image; in the image of God He created him; male and female He created them. (Genesis 1:26-27) New King James

Chapter 4

In the Life and Ministry of Jesus Christ, Grace and God's Goodness

As I opened the Human Anatomy Textbook to begin to read the chapter on the musculoskeletal system, there was great peace around me that took me right back into the same study of the skeletal bones; but this time without the turmoil. Within those same moments, I was told that there were some things that the Spirit of the Lord wanted to show me and was assigned to be my personal Teacher. I must admit, It really didn't matter at the time what I would be learning, only that I had complete confidence in the previous experience that had taken place within me to continue on with my anatomy lessons though the bone structure.

As we read the first paragraph together that related to the spinal column, I noticed that certain words appeared to illuminate with a glow within the text's description to catch my attention... *The spinal column is composed of a stack of 33 bones called vertebrae, divided into 5 distinct regions. In each region, the shape of the vertebrae is characteristic, as is the curve of the column.*

"Now consider the number thirty-three," my Teacher suggested. At first I was somewhat puzzled, but I knew that there had to be something significant about this particular number or it wouldn't have been brought to my attention. As I was encouraged to take a moment to think about the number thirty-three; I found myself surrendering to the fact that the number had to be of some Biblical significance....*and then a clearer understanding echoed into my ear, "This is about Jesus!"*

With this revelation given so clearly, I was immediately encouraged to open my Bible to read Luke chapter 3:21-23 for verification. What I found in these scriptures was, when Jesus was baptized by John, the Holy Spirit then descended in bodily form like a dove upon Him; and a voice came from heaven said, "You are my beloved Son; in You I am well pleased."

Soon after that in verse 23 it says, Now Jesus Himself began *His ministry* at **about thirty years of age**... (emphasis added).

As I held on that thought of **Jesus being thirty years old at that time**; I was then encourage to read on down to Luke chapter 4, verses 1and 2; Then Jesus being filled with the Holy Spirit, returned from the Jordan and was led by the Spirit into the wilderness, being tempted for forty days by the devil.

★The number *forty*'s biblical meanings are *Trials; Probation; Testing's!*

After the three temptations mentioned in verses 3 through 13; *the devil departed in defeat.* Jesus then returned to Galilee in the power of the Spirit. This was when **Jesus began His three-year ministry.**

★The number *three*'s Biblical meaning is *Divine completeness and perfection!*

Jesus's life and ministry totals up to thirty-three years up to the time of the crucifixion. The amazing thought of being led to discover a hidden design within all our spinal columns was definitely a brand new concept. An image of God that reflected a thirty-three year timeline of Jesus' years of life and ministry while He was here upon earth!

★The Biblical meaning of the number *thirty-three* is *"Promise!"*

Jesus was the **Promise** referred to throughout the whole Old Testament for all humanity!

By examining the spinal column diagram following this chapter, one can see that there are **thirty-three bones** from the top of the spinal column down to the bottom of the coccyx. This was the first secret image of God revealed at the start our study.

Clearly, God's image is reflected in Jesus' life and ministry. In John 14 verse 9 Jesus said, "He who has seen Me has seen the Father; so how can you say, 'Show us the Father'? Do you not believe that I am in the Father, and the Father in Me?

I did a little search of my own, and found that no other animal has the same count of vertebra in their spinal columns, not even the greatest of Apes down to the littlest monkey! Also, I found it interesting that the *five regions* of the human spine have a Biblical meaning through its numerical value too!

★The number *five's* meaning is that it *"completes the life and ministry of Jesus, with Grace; God's goodness"* (found through redemption).

The vertebral or spinal column within every human skeletal structure was, and still is today, cleverly made through a numerical design to represent symbolically Jesus' life and ministry upon the earth!

The Holy Spirit knew from the very start that the vertebral column (spinal column) was going to catch my attention. This was certainly the appropriate place to begin our eye-opening walk through the bone structure. The undisputed facts here are that; the spinal column is for the intended purposes of enabling man to stand upright physically as well as spiritually!

Also within the spinal column, is the most complex of nervous systems designed to flow through the center of the **twenty-four vertebrae** to all the organs in the human body and to each limb of the human body (arms, hands, legs and feet) to work in harmony with our brain.

★The number *twenty-four's* Biblical meaning is, *"The Priesthood!"*

Once again, there are *twenty-four* vertebrae starting from the cervical area, (neck bones C1-C7), of the spinal column down to the top of the sacrum designed to represent another one of God's images, the Priesthood. When we add the nine bones within the sacrum and the coccyx to the twenty-four there is a total of *thirty-three* bones. This symbolic numerical pattern has been there all along to reflect wholeness through the life of Jesus as the entire body works together in unity.

Genesis 1:26-27 certainly comes alive as we discover hidden secrets of God's Image!

Then God said, "Let Us make **man** in Our image_according to Our likeness; let them have dominion over the fish of the sea, over the birds of the air, and over the cattle, over all the earth and over every creeping thing that creeps on the earth."

So God created man in His *own* image; in the image of God He created him; male and female He created them. (Genesis 1:26-27)

★Take a look at the photo image of the spinal column that follows this chapter.

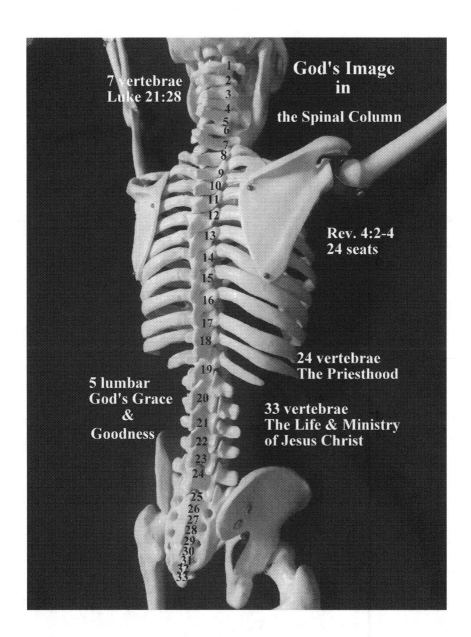

God's Image
in
the Spinal Column

7 vertebrae
Luke 21:28

Rev. 4:2-4
24 seats

24 vertebrae
The Priesthood

5 lumbar
God's Grace
&
Goodness

33 vertebrae
The Life & Ministry
of Jesus Christ

Chapter 5

The Resurrection, Spiritual Completeness and in the Father's Perfection

Within the text material, the next topic took us to the top of the spinal column. At the top of our spinal column are the neck bones. I then read over line that stated, *"and there are the first **seven** bones called; the cervical curvature* (C1–C7). Along with new awakening to Jesus' life and ministry, the Priesthood and to grace and redemption symbolically designed within our spinal column, I quickly had come to the conclusion that this was "definitely not" going to be a normal human anatomy lesson!

Within the words of the text, it stated that these *seven* cervical bones are flexible enough to allow the head to turn from side to side or to tilt the head backward or to bend the head forward. Here again, these *seven* cervical bones are at the top of our spinal column. These *seven* bones are the most flexible of all *the thirty-three bones* down through the design of our spinal column. (The seven cervical bones can be seen on the previous photo image of the spinal column).

I was then prompted by the leading of my personal Teacher to do a little research on the number *seven*. I discovered that the root of the name of the biblical number *seven* means; *the resurrection, spiritual completeness and in the father's perfection.*

Ever so gently, my Teacher was quick to remind me of the times I've gotten frustrated when I would try by to work out my own problems. I'm probably not too different from anyone else; I think we're all a little guilty of saving prayer as a last resort!

Jesus said, "Now when these things begin to happen, look up and lift up your heads, because your redemption draws near." (Luke 21:28)

Within this particular image of God, these *seven cervical bones* are designed in a way that a person is able to lift the head to look to Him during hard times. Through Jesus' words, He has given people His "word" to put to use for any situation. We must learn to trust the One who knows all and holds our destiny in His hands.

I was given a little more homework to do on the number *seven* and discovered that it is used with its numerical value by God at least 735 times throughout the Bible. It is used fifty-four times in the Book of Revelation alone. Here are just a few familiar examples of how God used the number *seven* in these scriptures:

Naaman was healed of leprosy after he dipped himself *seven* times in the Jordan. (II Kings 5:14) *Naaman experienced the resurrection power within his body when he was healed of the leprosy.*

The Lord told Joshua how to capture the city of Jericho. Even though Joshua could not see any logic in God's plan, by faith he obeyed. They were to march around the city, silently, for *seven* consecutive days. There were *seven* priests sent with the army to carry trumpets of rams' horns in front of the ark, and on the *seventh* day, the priests blew their horns, and the people shouted and the walls of the city fell down flat, then the armies of Israel took the city. (Joshua 6:14)

Peter asked Jesus how many times he should allow his brother to sin against him and still forgive him; seventy times *seven* was the answer Jesus gave Peter. (Matthew 18:21)

Also mentioned throughout the Book of Revelation, are the **seven** churches, the **seven** spirits, **seven** stars, **seven** seals, **seven** trumpets, and **seven** vials and so much more.

Thus the heavens and the earth, and all the host of them, were finished. And on the *seventh* day God ended His work which He had done; and He rested on the *seventh* day from all His work which He had done. Then God blessed the *seventh* day and sanctified it, because in it He rested from all His work which God created and made. (Genesis 2:1) "(emphasis added)."

It isn't hard to imagine that in everything God created and after He made man, He saw completeness and perfection! **Not only that but the resurrection**! I have to interject something about *the resurrection* at this point; the word says that God made man on the sixth day of creation.

I found this particularly interesting due to the fact;

★ The biblical number *six* has the meaning of *"Weakness of man; Manifestation of sin; Evils of Satan!"*

We all should find comfort in that, the number six was no surprise to our maker. God knew all about the number *six*. There can be no doubt that His divine plan was to make man on that particular day! And yet on the seventh day He rested because He saw all that He made was complete and perfect. We also can find rest in God's wisdom and foreknowledge; because the word *resurrection* is completeness and our Father's perfection is through Jesus' Redeeming Grace for all people through the cross and the resurrection.

Chapter 6

The Trinity and in the Fruits/ Gifts of the Spirit

As we read on to the next topic in the text, we found that at the bottom of our spinal column is the triangular shaped sacrum. There are **five** bones (S1 – S5) in the sacrum. Here again, the number *five* has the biblical meaning; *Grace and God's goodness*. These bones are described as being fused together. The textbook also described the sacrum as containing a large articular facet on either side. This *facet* is like a wing and is called the sacral *ala* (wing).

Then, I went on to read about the last bone below the sacrum, which is the **coccyx.** (I specifically remember this bone from injuring it so many times, referring it as *my tail bone*). This very small bone has a total of **four** bones (S6 – S9) designed within it. Interestingly, once again like the sacrum, the coccyx has its own *triangular* shape and like the sacrum the bones are fused together.

★ The biblical number *four* has the meaning *"of Creation; the world; Creative works!"*

I was then encouraged read Revelation 5:9. There are *four* living creatures that are connected with creation. These four living creatures have the symbolic representation for the hope of deliverance from the curse that is bound up with the blood-shedding of the coming Redeemer.

John witnessed and recorded these *four* living creatures along with the twenty-four elders as singing a new song and saying, "You are worthy to take the scroll, and to open its seals; for You were slain, and have redeemed us to God by Your blood out of very tribe and tongue and people and nation, and have made us kings and priests to our God; and we shall reign on the earth." (Revelation 5:9)

As we were looked at that this little bone just below the sacrum I realized the importance in its symbolic placement. Adam was the first temple made in God's Image with this prophetic design that signified all creation redeemed by the coming redeemer, Jesus the Christ, even before He had ever come to the earth through Holy conception! Our Great Almighty Creator; the Great I AM; the Alpha and Omega: How interesting! God's vision for His preplanned prophecy *to be fulfilled* was already designed within the spinal column of every man, woman and child!

The descriptions of these two bones are described in any medical dictionary as having triangular shapes. Of course immediately, the awareness of the Trinity came to mind.

As I did more research, I found that even though the word "Trinity" is a term not found in the Bible, it is still a word used to describe what is apparent about God in the Scriptures. The Bible does clearly refer to, God the Father, God the Son (Jesus Christ), and God the Holy Spirit, and also substantiates that there is only one God. So then, I discovered the term: *Tri* meaning three, *Unity* meaning one, Tri+Unity = Trinity. I discovered that the orthodox definition of the Trinity is described as *a three-fold personality existing in one divine being or substance; the union of one God of Father, Son, and Holy Spirit.*

Up to this point in our study, the life and ministry of Jesus Christ with the symbolic design up down our spinal column was certainly clear, and now, the Holy Spirit revealed the two triangular bones at the base of the spinal column. Both of these triangular bones are at the very foundation of our spinal column. How appropriate is that!

Even though the bones are fused together in each triangular shape they still allow for their total count of **nine**.

★The Biblical number *nine* has the meaning of *"completeness, finality, or fullness."*

Now, by adding these **nine** bones with the number **twenty-four** (the Priesthood) makes up the total number of **thirty-three,** biblically meaning the "Promise" are all within God's image. Clearly, it is not hard to add up the total for all the hidden secrets within God's Image thus far! (24+9=33)

To my amazement, I found each numerical bone count within our human spinal column consistent as well as significant within God's image.

Once again, the Holy Spirit took me back to review Genesis 1:26-27 as an important fundamental scripture.

Then God said, "Let Us make **man** in Our image according to Our likeness; let them have dominion over the fish of the sea, over the birds of the air, and over the cattle, over all the earth and over every creeping thing that creeps on the earth." So God created man in His *own* image; in the image of God He created him; male and female He created them. (Genesis 1:26-27)

It was certainly apparent to me at this point of our study, that the trinity within God's image was designed and placed in at least… these two triangular shapes representative of the **Father, Son, and Holy Spirit as tri-unity.** I had to stop for a moment to ponder over the importance of their triangular placements for the undergirding of the life and ministry of Jesus Christ, as well as representatives to the undergirding of our very own spiritual existence.

In the Fruits/Gifts of the Spirit

The Holy Spirit had revealed many of God's hidden secrets within our temple's foundation, but as we traveled up and then down the spinal column my childlike inquisitiveness grow even all the more. I knew deep inside my spirit that there had to be more hidden within the sacrum and the coccyx. On my way to church one evening, I just could not get those two triangular bones off my mind, so, I asked the Holy Spirit if there was something else secretly hidden there? The Holy Spirit responded in a whisper, **"Consider the nine fruits of the Spirit!"** Well, I had to pull off the side of the road! I don't know if it was because the Holy Spirit responded so quickly, or the fact that **nine** fruits of the spirit was an unexpected surprise. I then realized that I was sitting in my car awestruck in a vacant parking lot. Another hidden secret of God's image brought to my attention within our temple's foundation. How fearfully and wonderfully clever of Him!

But the fruit of the Spirit is love, joy, peace, long suffering, gentleness, goodness, faithfulness, gentleness, self-control. Against such there is no law. (Galatians 5:22-23)

I am convinced that the *nine fruits* of the spirit and the *nine gifts* of the spirit were designed to work together, so this would explain why God placed them together numerically within the sacrum and coccyx.

But the manifestation of the Spirit is given to each one for the profit *of all*: for one is given the word of wisdom through the Spirit, to another the word of knowledge through the same Spirit, to another faith by the same Spirit, to another gifts of healings by the same Spirit., to another working of miracles, to another prophecy, to another discerning of spirits, to another different kinds of tongues, to another the interpretation of tongues. But one and the same Spirit works all these things, distributing to each one individually as He wills. (I Corinthians 12:7-10)

These two vertebral bodies of bone were again symbolically and strategically placed by design at the foundation of our vertebral column by our Heavenly Father to show not only His image's within the trinity, but also the *nine* Fruits/Gifts of the his Holy Spirit.

★Again, the number *nine* gloriously shines on with the biblical meaning *of divine completeness from the Father.*

As God's Holy Spirit is allowed to fully resonate within His temples, *God's image of likeness will complete us* for a witness to others.

My eyes had become full of tears from the enlightenment being poured into my heart! The skeletal structure that I had been *weary of* most of my life had already taken on a whole new meaningful appearance. The symbolic bone placements of God's images that were revealed up to this point within my own body without even thinking about it, had begun to reshape my own concept of value and purposeful responsibilities deep down within my very own soul.

This was just the beginning of the Holy Spirit's invaluable tutoring, and believe it or not, this was the place in our study where I first realized that I was being given a firsthand visual walk through God's Temple!

And what agreement has the temple of God with idols? For you are the temple of the living God. As God has said, "I will dwell in them, and walk among them. I will be their God, and they shall be my people." (II Corinthians 6:16)

★Take a look at photo image of the sacral and coccyx bones and coccyx following this chapter.

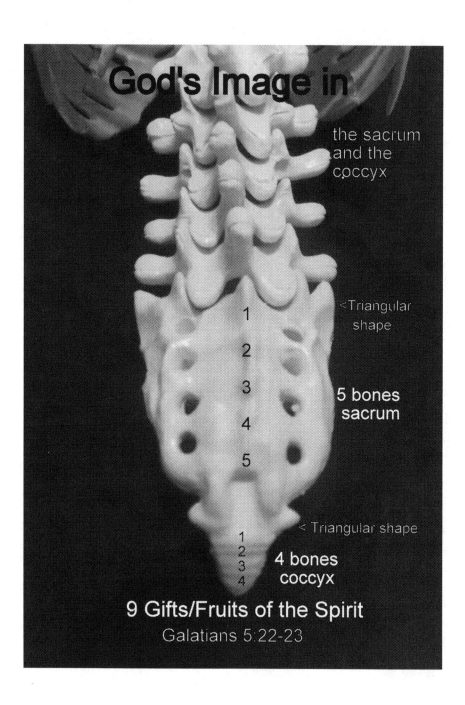

God's Image in the sacrum and the coccyx

< Triangular shape

5 bones sacrum

< Triangular shape

4 bones coccyx

9 Gifts/Fruits of the Spirit
Galatians 5:22-23

Chapter 7

The Thorns and the Kingdom of God

As we followed text material still within the spinal column, I was to keep in mind that there are *twenty-four* vertebral bones that stack one upon another from the top of the cervical curvature (C1 – C7) to the bottom of the lumbar curvature (L1 – L5). As I examined a single vertebral bone, I discovered that each of these bones is designed with a dorsal projection called a spinous process. These spinous projections can actually be felt if you run your fingers up and down your spine.

This Teacher impressed me to look up the word *spinous process* in my medical reference dictionary, and here is how the definition is written; *a short, sharp, **thorn–like** process of bone, a spinous process. The Greek word or Latin word for spine is spina or plural spinae. The Greek or Latin word for spina is: {L. **a thorn**, the backbone, spine}.*

It seemed clear to me to what the thorns represented, or at least I thought so at the time. God crafted a single thorn-like process of bone in each of the *twenty-four vertebrae* to be symbolic of the **crown of thorns** (notating again the number twenty-four meaning "The Priesthood"), that was mockingly placed on Jesus' head to symbolize "King of the Jews."

And they stripped Him and put a scarlet robe on Him. When they had twisted **the crown of thorns**, they put it on His head, and a reed in His right hand. And they bowed the knee before Him and mocked Him, saying, "Hail, King of the Jews!" (Matthew 27:28-29) "(emphasis added)"

Still yet, I was soon to discover another hidden secret of God's Image that concerned the thorns.

The Kingdom of God

Now when He (Jesus) **was asked by the Pharisees when the kingdom of God would come, He answered them and said,** "**The kingdom of God** does not come with observation; nor will they say, 'See here!' or 'See there!' **For indeed, the kingdom of God is within you."** (Luke 17:20-21) "(emphasis added)"

From Adam's made day, people have been designed with God's images formed from His very own blueprint. God's purpose was and still is for fellowship with His people and to be His completed spiritual dwelling place. Our temples were designed for His spirit to fill and to complete the kingdom of God within all His people. This entire concept explains why our enemy, Satan fights so hard to cripple and blind people into submission for his evil works.

On the road to Golgotha, the place of the skull where Jesus was crucified, Jesus was mockingly crowned King of the Jews by the governor's soldiers. The soldiers had constructed the prickly crown of thorns out of spite. Un-denounced to them, they were in fact performing an act of prophetic significance. (Matthew 27:28-29)

Along with the biblical meaning of the *number twenty four* that represents God's image in *"the Priesthood"*, the Holy Spirit quickened me to search more on the significance of **the thorn** and how it connects with the kingdom of God or Heaven.

Worldly Care

This is what was further revealed to me on this topic of the thorns. Through these next scriptures, the **thorn** was and will be found to represent worldly care and how the crown worn by Jesus made way to victory for the kingdom of God.

But He was pierced for our transgressions, He was bruised for our iniquities; the chastisement of our peace was upon Him. (Isaiah 53:5)

In Matthew 13:7, Jesus spoke in a parable about the seed that fell among the **thorns**, which grew up and choked the plants. *Here again, thorns represent worldly care.*

The apostle Paul wrote a warning against falling away from the faith; For the earth which drinks in the rain that often comes upon it, and bears herbs useful for those by whom it is cultivated, receives blessings from God (referring to people); **but if it produces thorns and brier, it is rejected and is near to being cursed.** (Hebrews 6:7-8) (emphasis added)

This scripture not only warns to end-time wrath, but Paul is addressing the unfruitfulness due to the cares of this world.

The apostle Paul brought out yet another interesting point that concerns **the thorn** in 2nd Corinthians chapter 12:7-9, And lest I should be exalted above measure by the abundance of the revelations, **a thorn in the flesh** was given to me, a messenger of Satan to buffet me, lest I be exalted above measure. Concerning this thing I pleaded with the Lord three times that it might depart from me. And He said to me, for "My grace is sufficient for you, for My strength is made perfect in weakness." Therefore most gladly I will rather boast in my infirmities, that the power of Christ may rest upon me. (emphasis added)

Again, I took note of Isaiah chapter 53: 5... But He was wounded for our transgressions, He was bruised for our iniquities; the chastisement for our peace was upon Him, and by His stripes we are healed.

The Holy Spirit has shown us in these scriptures that God has always loved people especially when we fail. Our Heavenly Father made special provision through Jesus suffering for His unmerited Grace; for all of our **sorrows caused by the thorns of life.** (Isaiah 53:4) (emphasis added)

Throughout our lifetime, the thorns of life have the ability to bring the believer, *and the nonbeliever,* to the place of recognizing ones physical and spiritual weaknesses. God wants each one of us to become as a little child with expectancy under the Kingdom of Heaven. Thy kingdom come thy will be done! Jesus wore the crown of thorns representing the Kingdom of God or Heaven made possible for us to enter because of his suffering.

Jesus said, "Assuredly, I say to you, unless you are converted and become as little children, you will by no means enter the kingdom of heaven. Therefore whoever humbles himself as this little child is the greatest in the kingdom of heaven." (Matthew 18:3-4)

Jesus not only paid the price for our sin on the cross, but He also bore our weakness. The everyday hindrances *through thorns or weaknesses* that we face daily are represented in the crown of thorns.

An interesting thought came to me, that for a fact, all four-legged animals have a backbone with a pattern of thorny bones on the anterior (outer side) of their spinal columns. God reigns over their own designs as well within their own circle of life, consider the sparrow! The difference between humans and four-legged animals is that our spinal column is designed to keep the human structure *standing upright* in spirit, built upon understanding. No other spinal column compares!

God's image, His temple is to *stand upright* spiritually as well as physically. God's people have been given authority to have dominion over all! God's image is designed within all people with the life and ministry of Jesus Christ. People born with spinal abnormalities are not exempt!!!

Then God said, "Let Us make **man** in Our image, according to Our likeness; let them have dominion over the fish of the sea, over the birds of the air, and over the cattle, over all the earth and over every creeping thing that creeps on the earth." So God created man in His *own* image; in the image of God He created him; male and female He created them. (Genesis 1:26-27)

★There is a photo image at the end of this chapter of a single vertebra

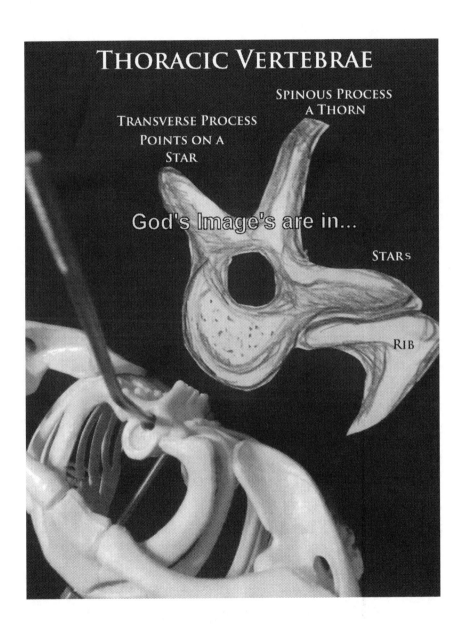

Chapter 8

Jesus' Birth and Bright and Morning Star

The next topic within the spinal column that we went on to study was the thoracic bones. This Teacher would not overlook any keys of information found in the text's description that related to design. And it really didn't take long for me to keep a close eye out for any descriptive wording that would be important within God's temple. Sure enough there was another hidden secret of God's image that would be discovered right below the seven cervical (neck) vertebrae. This is where the thoracic curvature begins, commonly known as our rib cage.

As we read the following paragraph, it described the design of each thoracic vertebra as having two points, side to side (laterally). These points are named, *transverse processes.* These side to side processes of bone are designed on each vertebra down to the sacrum. But, the first T1-T12 transverse processes lay directly behind each rib in our rib cage; these are made as connection points for each set of ribs. This design was found interesting because of the way it was described in the anatomy and physiology reference that contained the upcoming information.

Now I must admit this next description of the transverse processes was not found in any other reference material; nonetheless, coming thus far in our previous discoveries, all word descriptions had become relevant. Could God have placed the upcoming key word in the mind of the curriculum writer; quietly hidden there on purpose for this particular discovery? Maybe! To my surprise, here is how the transverse processes are described in the program text.

Transverse processes: These blunt projections arise laterally from the junction of the pedicle and the lamina, **like points on a star**, in the dorsal spine; they are articulations for the ribs. (*Laterally* meaning side to side; these *twenty four* blunt projections in all, are articulations for all twenty-four ribs. (The word *Articulation* means connecting together loosely to allow for movement).

★ Here again the biblical meaning of the number *twenty four* is in reference to "the Priesthood!"

As we looked more closely at the T1-T12 vertebrae, *points on a star* had unmistakably stood out like a beacon of light within our body's temple. I was most certainly confident in that this design was symbolic of the **Star of Bethlehem**; the sign of our Savior's birth. But, my Teacher pushed me on a little further to reference a few bible scriptures.

Not only does Matthew chapter 2:2 tell of the three wise men that traveled from the east of Jerusalem saying, "Where is He who has been born King of the Jews? For we have seen **His** *star* in the East and have come to worship Him." (emphasis added)

But, there is another reference to the foretelling of this **star** in the book of Numbers 24:17. Even though Balaam was known as a "cursing prophet," he fell prostrate on the ground as the Lord Almighty opened his eyes to this vision and prophesies, "I see Him, but not now; I behold Him, but not near; **A Star** will come out of Jacob; a Scepter will rise out of Israel…" (emphasis added)

This scripture is in reference to *a star* mentioned in Revelation 22:16, "I Jesus have sent My angel to testify unto you these things in the churches. I am the Root and the Offspring of David, and *the bright and Morning Star*." (emphasis added)

I have to believe through the words of my anatomy and physiology study, that God revealed Jesus as another image of Himself through an image of the *Bright and Morning Star,* and Oh, there is still more to come!

Go back to the photo image placed right after chapter 7. There you will see the transverse process (star) is on the diagram of the thoracic vertebrae.

Chapter 9

Priesthood and Governmental Perfection

Thus far, the walk up and down the human spinal column had miraculously shown hidden secrets of God's image through Jesus' birth, His 33-years of life and ministry, The Promise; also meaning Grace through Redemption, and The Kingdom of Heaven. Also, the symbolic designs of the fruits and gifts of God's own Holy Spirit!

Overwhelmed by these findings, I was ready to slow down to take in the findings shown so far, but the Holy Spirit seemed persistent about moving on into the thoracic cavity part of our lesson. As we promptly moved on to the bony thorax area or commonly known as our rib cage or thoracic cavity; the passage described this part of our skeletal anatomy as having 2 pair of 12 ribs that connect into the D1 down through the D12 vertebrae in the dorsal area of the spine. (Dorsal; pertaining to the back of the spine).

With miraculous wonder, I took an intense look at the rib cage, the bony thorax diagram! All sort of things swept through my mind about the biblical number twelve! The twelve disciples came to mind; the *twelve* tribes of Israel: The time when John was in the spirit he saw the Holy City of Jerusalem with the twelve pearl gates with the *twelve* foundations of the city with the *twelve* apostles names written on them described in the book of Revelations!

But my own thought pattern had come to a screeching halt as my Teacher abruptly interrupted my rambling notions. With stern encouragement to keep on reading, said, "Don't jump too far ahead of me; slowly read on a little further, I want to show you something!" My attention was then directed to a different topic within the bony thorax.

*Later, I was to discover that, the biblical number *twelve* has a meaning in reference to *"Perfect order or achieving governmental structural pattern: Simply put, Governmental Perfection."*

As I read on to the next paragraph about the **Sternum** or (breastbone), within the design of Sternum I discovered that it was described as having **three** parts: #1; The **Manubrium**, #2; the **Body**, and # 3, the **Xiphoid process**.

*The number *three* has the biblical meaning, "divine completeness!" (This number *three* is found throughout our body many times as we shall discover throughout our walk).

"Well now, how many times is the number **three** mentioned in the Bible," I asked? I certainly had a few ideas of my own, as one can only imagine: But the Holy Spirit gave no response, and then gently encouraged me to just keep on reading. Finally, the destination to where the Holy Spirit wanted us to arrive caused us both to stop and marvel at the full diagram of the human rib cage.

The diagram of the bony structure seemed to illuminate and rise from off the page with a soft glow that radiated through the bone structure showing off the ribs and the sternum. "Now... go back and reference the lesson material and I will guide you through with God's word," my Teacher instructed.

Not wanting to miss any of its details, I quickly went back to study the sternum. What I discovered was that at the very top portion of the sternum is the *manubrium*. There is a notch that you can actually feel at the base of your neck. This notch that is at the very top of one's manubrium is where your bony thorax starts. Next, I anxiously opened my medical dictionary for the reference information that concerned the *manubrium*. There I found its description that read something like this... *The portion of the sternum or of the malleus **that represents the handle**. [L. handle]...the upper segment of the sternum, a flattened, roughly **triangular bone**, occasionally fused with the body of the sternum...*

The abbreviation, L., used in the reference is noted as being a Latin word. Then I referenced another medical dictionary; the definition read like this...*a **handle-like structure** or part, such as the manubrium of the sternum*. The manubrium is another bone in our body that is described in the shape of a **triangle**. Here again, God's image of the Trinity was revealed through its description: The Father, Son (Jesus), and Holy Spirit. From the manubrium, I kept the word **handle** in mind. I then took a look at *the second part* of the sternum. I found that this bone is described in any medical dictionary as a long flat bone connecting with *the third part* of the sternum, called the *xiphoid* process.

Although we didn't intend to skip over the second bone of the sternum as important as it is, we did, and went on to study the xiphoid process. Here we discovered that the *xiphoid* process is shaped or designed once again, in the shape as a **triangle**. Again, there was a triangular shape of the Trinity, and of course this was my own thinking, but I was quickly encouraged to look further into a medical dictionary for the **xiphoid** bone's description.

This is what I discovered...*this xiphoid process bone as* [G. xiphos, sword!]....Interestingly, the word **xiphoid** derives from the Greek word xiphos for **straight sword**; the tip end of the body of the sternum.

★Take a look at the thoracic cavity to look at the shapes of the sternum that follows this right after this chapter!

Well it did not take a rocket scientist to identify what the Holy Spirit had revealed! At that very moment I called out, "Holy Spirit, you are showing me that there is a God image design of a **SWORD** in the middle of our thoracic cavity!!! THE WORD OF GOD IS... THE SWORD!** The Sword of the Spirit is the Word of God! The Word is God!"

I was then prompted to go to back to my Bible to reference John chapter 1 verse 1: **In the beginning was the *Word,* and the *Word* was with God, and the *Word* was God.** (emphasis added)

Then we went on down to verse 14: **And the *Word* became flesh** and dwelt among us, and we beheld His glory, the glory as of the only begotten of the Father, full of grace and truth. (emphasis added)

The next scripture we took a look at was Ephesians chapter 6:17: And take the helmet of salvation, **and the sword of the Spirit, which is *the word of God*.** (emphasis added)

Amazingly, the Holy Spirit had revealed another amazing image of God within the sternum! **The word of God, the Sword of the Spirit** cleverly shown to be a hidden secret of God's image in the center of the thoracic cavity directly over the heart of people!

At that same moment, I was not only captivated by this visual image given within the temple of our own body, but could tell that there was still much more to be revealed! I sensed that my Teacher was not through with this topic just yet, and was then given further instructions: "Now... go to the book of Revelation," the Holy Spirit instructed! "Read Revelation chapter 4:2 -4!" And so I did, and this is what John saw and how it is written...

Immediately I was in the Spirit; and behold, a throne set in heaven, and **One was sat on the throne.** And He who sat there was like a jasper and a sardius stone in appearance; and *there was* a rainbow round about the throne, in appearance like an emerald. Verse 4; Around the throne were **twenty-four thrones**; I saw **twenty-four elders** sitting, clothed in white robes; and they had on their heads crowns of gold on their heads. (emphasis added)

Here is what the Holy Spirit wanted to openly shed insight into: The bony thorax (rib cage) was designed by God and placed within His temple to be symbolic of Revelation 4:2 through verse 4! As John was in the Spirit he saw a throne set in heaven, and the ONE who sat on the throne. Here is another one of God's images designed and represented within the thoracic cavity of all people!

The two pairs of twelve ribs, twelve ribs on each side of the sternum, adding up to **twenty-four ribs**! Not only are the **twenty-four thrones or seats**, and elders represented, but John saw the **ONE** that sits on the throne, **Jesus, the Word of God represented by the three-part Sword!** God's image is the very **ONE** sitting on the throne of God! He, Jesus, is the Word, the SWORD of the SPIRIT along with the *twenty-four* thrones or seats with the twenty-four elders!

God's secret image is no longer hidden! It is alive through the biblical *number twelve's* meaning and is in reference to **Perfect Order or achieving governmental structural pattern, Governmental Perfection**!

This image of God is also within the biblical number *twenty-four's* meaning in reference with "The Priesthood, over heavenly government and heavenly worship"!

Once again I went back to read over John chapter 1:1, In the beginning was the Word, and the Word was with God, and the Word was God.

And John chapter 1:14, And the Word became flesh and dwelt among us, and we beheld His glory, the glory as of the only begotten of the Father, full of grace and truth.

And Ephesians chapter 6:17, And take the helmet of salvation, and the sword of the Spirit, which is the word of God.

Along with these hidden secrets of God's image, the Holy Spirit then directed me to go Ephesians chapter 2:20-22 ... having been built on the foundation of the apostles and prophets, Jesus Christ Himself being the chief cornerstone, in whom the whole building, being fitted together grows into a holy temple in the Lord, in whom you also are being built together for a dwelling place of God in the Spirit. (Ephesians 2:20-22)

These scriptures refer to our physical bodies as well as the Church body!

Having been captivated by each revealed secret of God's image thus far, I was reminded by my Teacher to reflect back again to the when God first designed and made Adam.

Adam's own skeletal structure had held these hidden secrets of God's image in Jesus' birth, life and ministry, and the Kingdom of God, God's image in the foundation of the apostles and the prophets, Jesus Christ himself being the chief cornerstone! God's image designed for the soul purpose of Ephesians chapter 2; 22, in whom you also are being built together for a dwelling place of God in the Spirit.

God's images within man have never changed to this day, which brings up an interesting point for instance, the Darwin theory. When we examine the thoracic cavity of the Neanderthal type man, the findings show that within the Neanderthal was found a rib count of nine on each side with a total count of eighteen ribs. Yes, we do know that the biblical number *nine* has the meaning of *divine completeness*! And that means even the Neanderthal type man was created under the *divine completeness* equal to an ape under Man's dominion like all the other, fish, birds, cattle and every other creeping thing on the earth according to Genesis 1:26-27!

★The Neanderthals rib count had a total number of eighteen with the biblical meaning of "**bondage**"!

★God's Image within Adam's rib count was purposely designed with a total number of twenty-four with the biblical meaning of "**the Priesthood**"!

In my opinion, I was never comfortable with the theory of evolution, and this gives me clarity and peace of mind! It was clearly understandable to me why the Holy Spirit had a deep heartfelt attraction for God's image cleverly locked within the thoracic cavity. And because of what was revealed there, I was reminded of Ephesians 3:20–22.

It is God's people that make up the church, which is built upon the apostles and the prophets, Jesus Christ himself being the chief cornerstone and we are still making preparation for the bridegroom.

For I am jealous for you with godly jealousy. For I have betrothed you to one husband, that I may present you as a chaste virgin to Christ. (II Corinthians 11:2) "(emphasis added)"

Do you not know that your bodies are members of Christ? Shall I then take the members of Christ and make them members of a harlot? Certainly not! (I Corinthians 6:15)

Or do you not know that your body is the temple of the Holy Spirit who is in you whom you have from God, and you are not your own? For you were bought at a price; therefore glorify God, in your body and in your spirit, which are God's. (I Corinthians 6: 19-20)

…For we are members of His body, of His flesh, and of *His bones*. (Ephesians 5:30)

★Take a look at the photo image of our thoracic cavity at the end of this chapter.

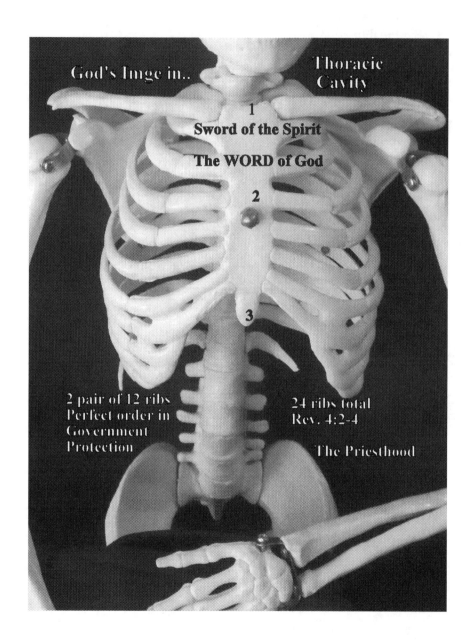

God's Imge in..

Thoracic
Cavity

1

Sword of the Spirit

The WORD of God

2

3

2 pair of 12 ribs
Perfect order in
Government
Protection

24 ribs total
Rev. 4:2-4

The Priesthood

Chapter 10

Wings resting and trusting

As hard as it was to move on; we walked on down to the pelvic girdle located just below the thoracic cavity. Within the pelvic girdle I discovered the number three once again. It wasn't hard to assume that the *number three* was symbolic of the Father, The Son and The Holy Spirit as well **as the biblical number meaning completeness and perfection**.

The pelvic girdle is described in any anatomy book as well as in my own text these three parts are; the ilium, the ischium, and the pubis. When we sit down our whole body rests on this bone called the pelvic girdle. The ilium part of the pelvic girdle spreads from one side to another and is described in any medical dictionary describes it like this: *The broad, flaring portion of the hip bone, distinct at birth but later becoming fused with the ischium and pubis; it consists of a body, which joins the pubis and portion, called the* **ala or wing**. **"Ala" is a Latin word for wing**.

The ilium can be felt when we place our hands on our hips while the pubis bone is on the bottom portion of the pelvic girdle. (Sometimes if there isn't enough padding on the buttocks and one sits very long on a hard surface, the pubis bone can be felt and can make one most uncomfortable). Within the pelvic girdle is a second set of wings. This second set of wings is called false pelvis.

★There is a photo diagram of the Pelvic Girdle at the end of this chapter.

By looking at the pelvic diagram that follows this chapter, we can plainly see that we have a #1 in large set of wings within our skeletal structure that is designed to function as a *resting bone* for our body to sit. The #2 marked as second set wings outlined for clarity inside the pelvic girdle was designed to protect the reproductive organs, as well as the bladder, etc.

I love this prayer of David as he pleads to be hidden under the shadow of God's wings from those who wish to harm him. In Psalms chapter 17:8-9 David prayed … Keep me as the apple of the eye, hide me under the shadow of thy wings, verse 9, From the wicked that oppress me, from my deadly enemies, who compass me about.

God's image within the wings of pelvic girdle is His very own design of hidden protection for new life, as he or she develops within their mother's womb.

He shall cover you with His feathers, and under **His wings you shall take refuge...** (Psalms 91:4) (emphasis added)

He that dwells in the secret place of the Most High shall abide under the shadow of the **Almighty**. (Psalms 91:1) Here again, God's image in the wings!

Within our skeletal design, the iliac wings is the symbolic design of God's image representative of resting and trusting in our God for safety; no matter the trouble that we are going through. Every one of us must learn to rest upon, and in, His wings of protection through God's written promises. God is our refuge.

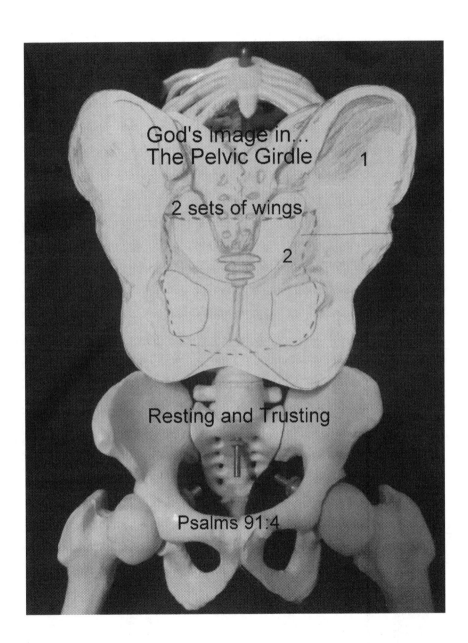

Chapter 11

Under His wings and shields of protection

The next topic within our body's bone structure to study was the scapulae. On examination I found that there are two matching scapulae (pl.). Within the descriptive information along with what I discovered in a medical dictionary revealed once again clues that would reveal God's image.

As directed by my Teacher, I went on to take a closer look into what the reference dictionary had to say about the scapulae. The definition was written like this…*A **large triangular** flattened bone lying over the ribs, posteriorly on either side, articulating laterally with the clavicle at the acromioclavicular joint and the humerus at the glenohumeral joint. It forms a functional joint with the chest wall, etc.*

There are indeed two of these unique bones designs placed on the backside of our thoracic cavity. When I inspected both scapulae carefully, I realized that they really are triangular shaped, on each side of our upper spinal column, right and left. By their unique placements with their triangular designs, each scapula lies flat inwardly toward the spinal column, then reaches down to the seventh rib on each side. You can look at the photo image at that follows this chapter.

★The biblical number *two* has the meaning of *union*.
★And the biblical number seven has the meaning of *Resurrection; Spiritual completeness; Father's perfection.*

The Holy Spirit made it quite easy to see that each scapula bone is/was of God's own design made to represent His image in the shields of **perfection** that lie across the upper back sides of our rib cage where God's image is seen in Revelations 4:2-4; *The Priesthood and Governmental Perfection, and the Sword of the Spirit.*

These bones were designed by our Heavenly Father with His image to mirror Himself as shields of protection in His perfection. The two triangular shields (The Father, Son and Holy Spirit working as one in union) are as being wings of protection for the mental or physical escape that work in the defense of God's designed Temple, or both!

David described God as the Sovereign Savior when he wrote; For by You I can run against a troop, by my God I can leap over a wall. *As for* **God, His way is perfect**; the word of the LORD is proven**; He is a shield to all who trust in Him**. (Psalm 18:29-30) (emphasis added)

David wrote in Psalm 91:2-4, I will say of the LORD, "*He is* my refuge and my fortress; My God, in Him I will trust." Surely He shall deliver you from snare of the fowler *and* from the perilous pestilence. He shall cover you with His feathers, and under His wings you shall take refuge; His truth *shall be your* shield and buckler."

Indeed, as God's people learn to walk in the truth of God's word we are *protected* and we will experience His truth as our *shield of perfection*. The scapulae bones within our skeletal structure symbolically represent **God's image as our shields of protection covered with His wings of refuge.**

Paul wrote in, Ephesians chapter 6:16, above all, taking the *shield of faith* with which you will be able to quench all the fiery darts of the wicked one. (emphasis added)

★ Look at the photo image of the scapulae at the end of this chapter.

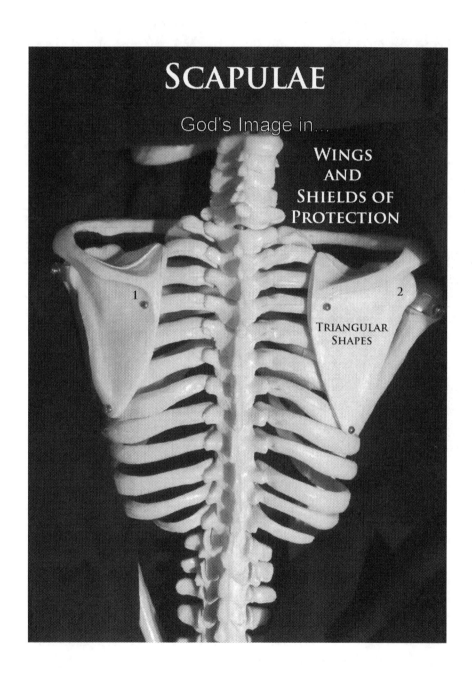

SCAPULAE

God's Image in...

**WINGS
AND
SHIELDS OF
PROTECTION**

1

2

**TRIANGULAR
SHAPES**

Chapter 12

The Cross of Redemption

As the Holy Spirit walked me back to the front of the skeletal anatomy, I had already grown to anticipate God's image within every aspect of our bone structure. In saying that, I somehow would have been disappointed if there had not been a hidden secret within the design of our clavicle bones.

To start off with, the clavicle bones are two bones that we commonly refer to as our right and left collar bones. These two bones can be easily felt with your finger tips by pressing lightly starting at the top of the sternum and follow the bones from side to side to each shoulder. These clavicle bones connected to our right and left scapula bones which complete the structure of our skeletal shoulders.

On careful examination of these two bones in the diagram, I was to take special notice as to the way these two bones connect with the manubrium; one bone extending from each side, right to left.

I was then instructed by my Teacher to set aside for a moment the design of *the clavicles* for a quick review of our three-part sternum. By doing so, the sternum in which was designed to show the Sword of the Spirit, and the Word of God (Jesus) had become particularly interesting! As we took a closer look at the design of the *clavicle bones* and how they were placed to connect with the manubrium; these bone placements took on another breath taking visual within God's image!

The Holy Spirit opened my eyes to see the complete picture of *Jesus, the Word of God, the Sword of the Spirit* designed within our three-part sternum with His out stretched arms as of His body on the cross! The very idea of this image was a whole lot breathtaking indeed! A hidden secret of God's image with His symbolic design revealing His redemptive love for all mankind! In this design, *revealing God's preplanned redeeming Grace through the cross of Jesus Christ His only Son!*

This image of God has been anchored securely within the middle of our temple's chest bone from the beginning! Imagine that! And it's placed right over our very heart beat! Just think of it again: God's preplanned redemption through His only Son, Jesus!

★Look at the photo image of the clavicles that follows this chapter.

Time seemed to stand still for a moment as this Teacher expounded upon the depth of God's never changing love for all people. Here, the Holy Spirit had revealed a symbolic design within the I Corinthian 6:19 temple's foundation, locked within our body's bones! God had already set up His predestined plan for man's needed redemption and it was first designed within Adam and Eve. It's no wonder God could rest on the seventh day from everything He created and made. In Genesis 1:31 it is written; Then God saw everything that He had made, and indeed it *was* very good.

As a review, this was certainly a good place for me to stop and walk through the sternum again as described in Chapter 9… the sword of the spirit; the word of God; Jesus, *and now the clavicle bones* that represent Jesus' arms. The clavicle bones extend from the symbolic image of Jesus, from *the three-part sternum.*

For a moment, I had to think about this hidden design within the temple of our body. Here is a spiritual bone design that shines God's image in a three-fold picture!

1. God's image in the throne that is referred to in Revelation 4:2-4,
2. God's image in the plan of redemption by way of the cross,
3. The Holy Spirit who raised Jesus from His death to life again.

I was reminded by my Teacher that there are "many gods" in this world that many people yield, to sooth their own hearts desires. But those who serve them die with them because they are deceived by Satan. It is only the Holy Spirit of the One and True God who raises us up to life again after our earthly death, so that we can live eternally in Heaven.

But if the Spirit of Him who raised up Jesus from the dead dwells in you, He who raised Christ from the dead will also give life to your mortal bodies through His Spirit who dwells in you. (Romans 8:11)

Jesus the Christ's unselfish sacrifice for all humanity explains His deserving reverence. Jesus is the One who sits on the throne described in Revelations 4:2-4. He rules and reins in Lordship with His Father in the center of the twenty-four seats of the twenty-four elders, as well as knocking on our heart's door for Him to be the Lord of our spiritual heart. But he who is joined to the Lord is one spirit *with Him*. Flee sexual immorality. Every sin that a man does is outside the body, but he who commits sexual immorality sins against his own body. **Or do you not that your body is the temple of the Holy Spirit *who* in is in you, whom, you have from God, and you are not your own?** **For you were bought at a price;** therefore glorify God in your body, and in your spirit, which are God's. (I Corinthians 6:17-20) (emphasis added)

Jesus paid the highest price for our redemption through His shed blood. You see, *the life giving blood* within Jesus *was not* of His earthly father, Joseph, but of His Heavenly Father, the Most High God! Mary, Jesus' mother, conceived life within her womb by the Spirit of God, which made God His Heavenly Father!

This is the spiritual miracle **of God's Blood** through Jesus that is "eternally victorious" over the common blood within mortal man! When we come to the decision to receive Jesus Christ as our personal Savior and Lord, that same Holy Spirit *gives us the spirit of adoption through the blood of Jesus; His Heavenly Father's BLOOD!* **His LIFE BLOOD for ETERNAL LIFE!**

Satanists, who take part in sacrificial practices to Satan, counterfeit the truth when they use the blood of animals and even the blood of humans; this practice is deceitful to ETERNAL DEATH! A horrible, hellish eternal life separated from Glorious Eternal Life in Heaven! **Because the Heavenly Father's Life Blood is not in it**!

If you have not already, please just simply ask God to forgive you of all your past sins, and acknowledge that Jesus paid for your redemption on the cross. Then invite the Holy Spirit's presence to come and dwell within your "God designed Temple!"

God's image is in our LIFE BLOOD because of OUR BONES

Our bones provide a hard framework to support all our soft organs. Within our study, I learned that our bone structure is an organ too! Just like our lungs, stomach, liver, pancreas, kidneys, reproductive organs etc. Up until this study, I had always believed them to be just hard on the outside with bone morrow on the inside. I was somewhat surprised to discover that there is a whole lot more. Even while our bones are hard on the outside; our bones contain nerve tissue, cartilage, and muscles. There are also fibrous connective tissues for blood vessels to run through our bones. No wonder when we break a bone, it takes a while to heal. There is a lot in there that has to mend.

I was still to discover that God designed our bones to have *five* different functions. *(He has surely given us Grace and His Goodness).* **The first function we will look at is for Blood**

Cell Formation. Within the marrow cavities inside our bones is where our blood cells are formed. There are areas of spongy bone where blood formation takes place. There are little blood vessels within the marrow or spongy bone that run through the cartilage of our bones that are continually replenishing our *life's blood*. This *life blood* keeps the temple of our body from becoming anemic, weak and frail. An important message learned here is to take care of your bones!

The other four functions of our bones are:

1. **Our bones support** and cradle our soft organs.
2. **Our bones protect**, for instance our brain is secured within the bones of our skull, our ribcage protects our lungs, stomach, etc., and our spinal bones protect our spinal cord.
3. Our muscles connected by tendons are attached to **our bones for proper movements** of our body parts, like breathing, walking, and using our arms and hands. Movements that we take for granted sometimes.
4. **Our bones store many minerals**. The biggies are Calcium and phosphate. Our bones is like a bank, working constantly with deposits made from good nutrition and withdraws made to other areas in our body where needed for proper function too!

We have the *long bones* of our arms and legs; *short bones* in areas like our wrists and ankles; *flat bones* like in our sternum; ribs and skull bones; *and irregular bones* like in our hips and in our vertebrae. These *four* different shapes of bone, even though designed differently, make their own levels of contribution for the formation of blood cells.

*Here is God's image again in the biblical *number four* meaning: *Creation; The world; Creative works.*

Our Heavenly Father's seed Blood is eternal life though Jesus Christ. And His image in our blood sustains our bodies with ongoing life while here on this earth. His image is still in the BLOOD!

Adam's Special Birthday

The Holy Spirit, our Teacher was gracious to shine His light over God's image first placed within Adam's bones. Adam was given a special "Birth-day" with divine purpose. Adam's birthday was on the sixth day of creation. The sixth day of man's creation with its numerical meaning was by NO mistake. God had already taken in account for Adam's sin and our sins.

God had His own carefully thought out plan for redemption as He spoke with those around Him on 'Adam's Special Birthday', when God said, "Let Us make man in our image…" in Genesis 1:26, He went right to work with His clever design. His image design went within the clavicles and sternum with Jesus on the cross. When God said, "Let Us make man in our image…God knew that it would take the redeeming BLOOD of His only Son, Jesus, the Sword of the Spirit. And Jesus did not disappoint His Father!

For God so loved the world that He gave His only begotten Son, that whoever believes in Him should not perish but have everlasting life. For God did not send His Son into the world to condemn the world, but that the world through Him might be saved. (John 3: 16-17)

You see, the ★The *number six* has the Biblical meaning of the Weakness of man; Manifestation of sin; Evils of Satan.

God's image had predestined to cover all sin! His hidden secret was first designed within Adam! After all, God rested on the seventh day. In the heavens and on the earth God's completeness was God's perfection!

Once again, the Holy Spirit took me back to review Genesis 1:26-27 as an important fundamental scripture. God said, "**Let Us**

make man in Our image, according to Our likeness, and let them rule over the fish and of the sea and the birds of the air." So God created man in His own image; **in the image of God He created him**; male and female He created them. "(emphasis added)."

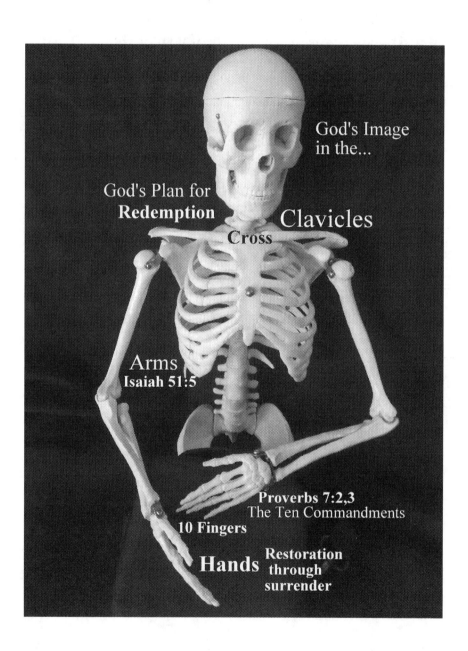

Chapter 13

Divine Completeness and Perfection

Next we walked on further to examine the upper extremities, which are the skeletal arms. The right and left humerus bones are the first bones that are connected to adjoining points where our shoulders meet, as with the right and left scapula (*shield, wings*). This area is also directly beneath where the clavicle bones (*the cross*) also adjoin to the upper two scapulae. One can actually feel where the clavicle and upper scapula meet at the top of ones shoulders. (There is a photo image at the end of chapter 12)

As we studied the skeletal structure of the arms we found that there are a total of *three* bones in our skeletal temple's arms (*God's image of His divine completeness and perfection*). The *three* bones in each arm are the *humerus* bone, **the radius**, and the *ulna*. All three of our arm bones are designed to work in unity just as the Father, Son, and The Holy Spirit do!

As a side note: There are seven landmarks where the ligaments and muscles are attached for proper flexibility and movement. Once again the biblical meaning of the *number seven* is *Resurrection; Spiritual completeness; Father's perfection*

OH, sing unto the LORD a new song! For He hath done marvelous things; **His right hand and His holy arm**, have gained Him victory. (Psalms 98:1) (emphasis added)

Interestingly, the discovery of the Latin word for **radius** is *wheel, rod, and ray*. There is a radius bone in each arm. Jeremiah

18 verse 3 describes what Jeremiah saw when he was instructed to go down to the potter's house. While there he saw how the **potter brought forth work on the wheels**. Ezekiel described **the cherubim's moving about on wheels** and God's Glory in Ezekiel chapter 10.

We must keep in mind; God's arms are continuing to judge the people and the islands based on careless decisions that do not protect Israel.

The Lower Extremities

Walking on down to our skeletal legs it is clear to see that there are three bones in each lower extremity. The first bones in the upper lower extremities are the femurs. The femur bone or our thigh is the largest and strongest bone at the top of both our legs. Then right below the knees is the tibia and the **fibula** bones. Interestingly, the Latin description in any medical dictionary for the fibula bone is "*buckle*".

He shall cover thee with His feathers, and under His wings you shall take refuge; His truth *shall be your* shield and **buckler**. (Psalms 91:4) (emphasis added)

As we trust God's promises by acting on His Word, His truth becomes our shield and our buckler. A **buckler** is a spike that sticks out from the center of a shield making it an offensive weapon as well as for a defensive one. God is our strength. He is our deliverer. He is our shield and He fights for us.

It is interesting that in this verse, these weapons; the shield, buckles, feathers, relates to war and used for our defense during battles. These are coupled with a beautiful picture **image of God in our very bones** as a mother hen that shelters her chicks under His wings. He protects us just like a protective mother hen protects her young when we trust Him. His truth is our shield and buckler. Trust God by trusting His Word.

Within each skeletal leg there is the total of *three* bones all working together, once again. All *three* work together as one. *God's image designed with completeness in mind.* An interesting note here is that there are seven landmarks located on the lower extremity bones to where the muscles and ligaments are attached for proper mobility and function: as previously discovered in the upper arm skeletal structure. This design allows for proper flexibility and movement of the muscles and ligaments so that the legs can move smoothly in unison keeping our upright postural balance.

Feet and Arches

We traveled on down to the lower extremities of our leg bones to our feet. Here we discovered that each foot and ankle has seven #7 tarsal bones *(spiritual completeness, our father's image of perfection)*, five metatarsal bones *(the image of God's Grace)* and fourteen phalanges.

★The number *fourteen's* biblical meaning is, *"Deliverance" as well as "Salvation."*

These fourteen bones were designed to provide a forward thrust as man is designed to *walk upright* in deliverance because of our salvation purchased through Jesus Christ, our Lord!

Note: (Four-legged animals have tarsal bones that point upward and to the back of their feet for moving about on all fours).

The steps of a *good* man are ordered by the LORD, and He delights in his way. Though he fall, he shall not be utterly cast down; for the LORD upholds *him with* His hand. (Psalms 37:23, 24)

One of my favorite scriptures is in Psalms 119 verse 133, Direct my steps by Your word, and let no iniquity have dominion over me.

As we studied each foot, another interesting design was found. Each foot contains **three arches.** They are the *medial arch, the lateral arch* and the *transverse arch*; all *three* are found only to be completed with their muscle tissue. These **three arches** maintain the body's structural stability. These three arches are not within our bone design, but this information was important enough to add in as an extra bonus!

Until this study, I never knew that God designed three arches in the foot. In the past, I've heard the phrase often used, "fallen arches," but I had always thought that people had only two arches. Well... there is that biblical number three again, *divine completeness and perfection*! These three arches in each foot's design maintain the body's structural stability.

Our musculoskeletal structure has six arches altogether; Oh, *six*, the number of man. I sure am thankful for the revelation of God's perfect plan to redeem us from our weaknesses that causes us to sin from the very beginning.

★The biblical number six *represents the weakness of man and manifestation of sin*; *Evils of Satan*.

Take a moment and reflect on what was revealed in chapter 9, about the Kingdom of Heaven and the criteria to walk in it. God knew all along that Jesus would pay the ultimate price with His shed blood for our weaknesses. Jesus paid for it all on the cross. When we do stumble we are picked up and encouraged to move on, we are God's temples! (Psalms 37:23)

I found it interesting too, that there are 7,000 nerves in each foot. Here again, the *number seven* meaning, is *Resurrection; Spiritual completeness; Father's perfection*. Fourteen thousand nerves in both feet: God's image in *deliverance and salvation*! God is so good! God loves me and God surely loves you!

The steps of a *good* man are ordered by the LORD, and He delights in his way. (Psalms 37:23)

God's ways are perfect!

★ See the photo image of the legs and feet following this chapter.

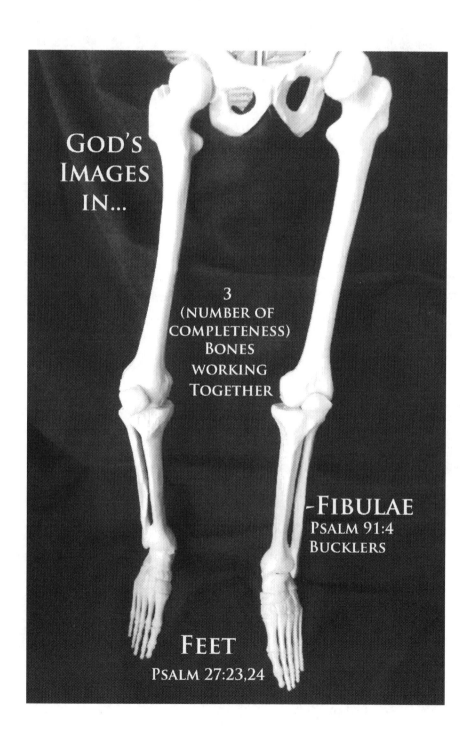

GOD'S IMAGES IN...

3
(NUMBER OF
COMPLETENESS)
BONES
WORKING
TOGETHER

-FIBULAE
PSALM 91:4
BUCKLERS

FEET
PSALM 27:23,24

Chapter 14

God's Law, Government and Restoration through Surrender

As we traveled back up to the arms, we studied the skeletal hands. Each of our hands has *three* groups of bones: The carpal-wrist, metacarpal-hand, phalanges-digits (fingers).

The number three stands for *"that which is complete."* We must not forget that *God's characteristic image* is *complete* through the number three; and they are omniscience (all knowing), omnipresent (ever-present) and omnipotence (al-mighty).

The very nature of man is made up of three parts; body, soul and spirit that ultimately makes up mans *complete nature.* God also gives man a *complete gift* packaged in faith, hope and love; and how about the three great divisions of *completing time* of the past, present and future.

By looking at your own hand, one can see that there are five fingers on each hand.

★The biblical number *five* represents *God's image of Grace, Peace, and Protection.*

By adding up on both hands it's not hard to see that there are ten fingers altogether.

*★The number *ten* is biblically viewed to *symbolically represent law, government, and restoration.*

By taking into account God's image in *the numbers five and ten*, and by living and serving *by God's law, government, and restoration,* we can have *Grace, Peace, and Protection* within the temples of our own bodies. This is an amazing visual of God's image. Consider the Ten Commandments; Keep my commands and live, and my law as the apple of your eye. **Bind them on your fingers**; write them on the tablet of your heart. (Proverbs 7:2,3) NKJ (emphasis added)

The Ten Commandments

1. You shall have no other gods before Me.
2. You shall not worship any graven image.
3. You shall not take the name of the Lord your God in vain
4. Observe the Sabbath day, to keep it holy
5. Honor your father and your mother
6. You shall not murder.
7. You shall not seal
8. You shall not bear false witness
9. You shall not bear false witness against your neighbor
10. You shall not covet

Within God's Temple (proof discovered through visual design) we abide by only one set of Laws in government, and they rest upon God's Son.

Isaiah 9:6 mentions five names given to Jesus, they are:

1. Wonderful
2. Counselor,
3. The Mighty God
4. The Everlasting Father

5.   The Prince of Peace.

Isaiah 9:6 and 7 are written like this; For unto us a Child is born, unto us a Son is given: and the government will be upon His shoulder. And His name will be called Wonderful, Counselor, Mighty God, Everlasting Father, Prince of Peace.

Of the increase of His government and peace *there will be* no end, upon the throne of David and over His kingdom, to order it and establish it with judgment and justice from that time forward, even forever. The zeal of the LORD of hosts will perform this.

Jesus is restoration, and the fingers on our very hands symbolically represent God's image as doing things according to the Kingdom of Heaven for His service.

The apostle Paul wrote in his letter to Timothy: I desire therefore that the men pray everywhere, lifting up holy hands, without wrath and doubting… (I Timothy 2:8)

Prayer with the lifting up of holy hands has always been customary among the Jews and even among the heathen. The hands were also lifted and spread out toward heaven *as a posture of surrender.*

In I Timothy 4:14, Paul encouraged Timothy to not neglect the gift that was in him. The elders of Lconium and Lystra laid hands on Timothy and prophesied concerning the gifts and purposes of God given for his life.

The laying-on of hands, with prophecy is one of the means by which the Holy Spirit employs to reveal His will and purposes to His servants. Paul urged Timothy to exercise his gift. The same Holy Spirit with the same message is for us today. (There is a photo image of the arms and hands at the end of chapter 12)

With the enlightenment given on the meaning of the biblical number ten, it is not hard to believe that if all Godly people would surrender with up-lifted holy hands and repent of our sins and of our nation's sins, what great things could we dare imagine God would do in lieu of our world's economic crises and ungodly corruption! God will heal our Land!

In this next section is an interesting overview of our finger nails and toenails. Again, each nail is completed by having *three parts*: The root of the nail, the body (where the nail is attached), and bed-under the nail. We don't usually see the bed under the nail unless the nail is damaged and comes off.

★Once again, the biblical meaning of the number three stands for *"that which is complete."*

We must not forget that the characteristics of God's images are *complete* in the number three; and they are omniscience (all knowing), omnipresent (ever-present) and omnipotence (al-mighty).

★ Turn back to the end of chapter 12 and look at the photo image of the arms and hands.

Chapter 15

The Temple's Sanctuary

The human skull has been horribly misunderstood as we all have seen it in countless ways, artfully counterfeited with darkness and evil. As I reflect back to the beginning of our study together; those might very well have been the reasons why I flipped hurriedly past the bony expression. No matter, the amazing enlightenment that the Holy Spirit has already walked me through up to this point had surely laid enough fertile ground for the trip back to the human skull to discover its own hidden secrets locked inside.

As we went back to study the human skull, I realized because of our walk through our bone structure, a genuine smile on the front of the human skulls face. WOW! God's image with a pleasant smile of satisfaction, a joyful countenance that I will never look over again! The very thought of God's smile after He had made Adam. God, Jesus, the Holy Spirits image along with all the others must have made God pleased at his design; completed in God's eyes.

I must admit that within the human skull is a revelation given to me only in part. But for every Bible Scholar that has studied the tabernacle of the Old Testament, he or she might find the human skull sanctuary most intriguing. The Holy Spirit was so good to hang with me until the end of our walk and I am thankful even for the enlightenment that I know only scrapes the surface of its contents.

Now, before I even attempted to walk through God's designed human skull where our own temple's sanctuary is, I was instructed to first take a look into its preparatory use.

The first known tabernacle sanctuary described in the Book of Exodus 25 starting with verse 1, where God spoke to Moses and told him to speak to the children of Israel about bringing in **their best of their heart offerings**; their gold, silver, brass, fine linens of blue, purple and scarlet; goats' hair, ram skins dyed red, badgers' skins and shittim wood, oil for light, spices for anointing oil and sweet incense, onyx stones and precious stones for the ephod (high priests' garment), and in the breast plate: All to make God a sanctuary so that He could dwell with them.

In this passage of scripture, it is not hard to understand that God had a purpose in mind when He asked for the children of Israel to give their first fruit offerings as their sacrificial worship. He wanted their offerings to come from their heart. By asking this of the children of Israel, their heartfelt offerings created a place of love and adoration conducive for God's spirit to dwell with his people.

Then God instructed in Exodus 25 verse 9, According to all that I show you, *that is,* the pattern of the tabernacle, and the pattern of all its furnishings, just so you shall make *it.*

The fundamental principle that God gave to Moses and the children of Israel was carried over years later for the design of King Solomon's Temple.

Today, because of our privileged walk through, *The Temple of Our Own Body,* we will discover that within the human skull are various similarities that will indeed correspond with God's design of the first tabernacle sanctuary given to Moses.

As we studied the human skull, I found that there are **three layers of bone** that surround the skull its self symbolically meaning, *divine completeness and perfection.* The cranium and has been designed within God's image being made up of **eight flat bones**.

*The number *eight* has the biblical meaning of *"New Birth or New Beginnings"*.

Inside the cranium is an area composed of the *calvaria and the base of the skull*. What was revealed by my Teacher in this area of the calvaria through any medical description is most interesting! Inside the calvaria is an inner surface of compact bone that is actually called an **inner table**. The inner table of the skull is compact layers of bone that covers the brain.

The outer surface of the calvaria is called the **outer table**. This outer table of the skull is compact layers of bone that covers the brain on the outside. Between the two tables is a spongy bone that makes up the thickness of the calvaria.

Again, similarities in tabernacle design! Around the skull... these three layers of bone represent three compartments of the tabernacle:

1. The Holy of Holies
2. The Holy Place
3. The Outer Court

The rounded area of the skull is designed to protect the human brain and the special sense organs, which enables us to smell, taste, etc. This is a bony case called the cranium.

There is also a sphenoid bone that forms the base of the skull, which was described in my text material likened too as the *wings of an eagle*. In the **outer table** of the base of the skull are **the greater wings** of the sphenoid, and **the lesser wings are on the inner table** of the base of the skull.

The *greater wings* are the lateral projections of the sphenoid body that forms the outer wall of the orbits. (Each side, left to right wing is designed behind our eyes and forms with the outer table of the skull.)

Lesser wings – thin, triangular projection from upper part of sphenoid body forms posterior part of roof of orbit that same as *the inner table* of the base of the skull.

Now as we consider the mercy seat within the Old Testament tabernacle sanctuary inside the Holies of Holies; there are **two sets of Cherubim's wings** over the mercy seat. Between the **two sets of wings is where God spoke** to the priests of those days.

Well now, this brought me to the point that I had to consider where God's voice is heard inside our temple's sanctuary? That's right, somewhere between the two sets of wings within our temple's sanctuary. This must mean that even the **Cherubim's are within God's image.** All, are designed within our own temple's sanctuary! **The Mercy Seat within the OT tabernacle was a precious piece of furniture that represented Jesus' finished work.** As we think about it, from all the hidden secrets of God's image that has come to light from the Holy Spirit by God's own hand and Son, the work was finished for us individually through the blood that Jesus shed on Calvary's Cross. It's kind of breathtaking to realize that God's personal sanctuary concept was *first* patterned within Adam's boney skull!

Let's take a peek at a couple of *important life-changing evidences* **of the** *Holy Spirit's work.*

Altar of burnt offering: The altar of burnt offering is a graphic symbol of the *ultimate reality* of Calvary through Jesus Christ!

The laver of bronze: The laver of bronze is actually symbolic of *the very next steps forward into our Christian walk.*

★See the photo image of the inner skull that follows this chapter.

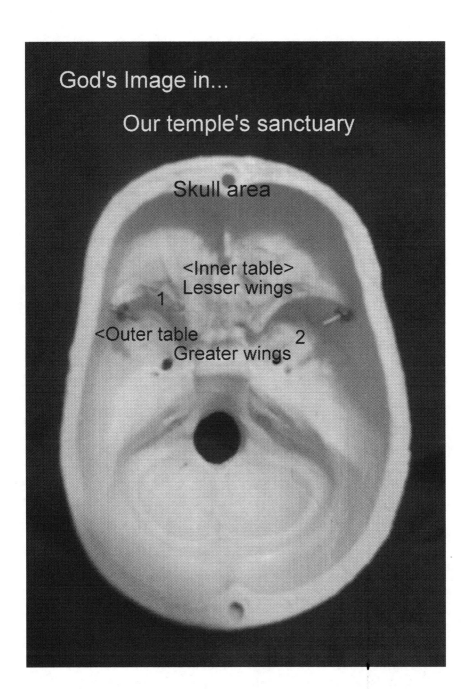

Chapter 16

Gate of the Temple

The Holy Spirit pulled me back into the middle ear, I then realized why. There were *three interesting bones* that my Teacher wanted me to review.

My homework was to reference my medical dictionary for the symbolic meanings, of the *malleus, incus,* and *stapes.* Each of these bones held hidden secrets of spiritual importance. During my research, I found that each bone had a Latin description attached. These Latin descriptions can be found in about any medical dictionary.

This is how the descriptions of three symbolic bones were given (remember, there are only *three bones* in the middle of each ear). Again, these three bones are named for their shapes: malleus, incus, and stapes.

*Once again, the biblical number *three* means: *Divine completeness and perfection.*

When I referenced the first bone, malleus, I discovered that there is a descriptive word used for it in the dictionary, and it is... syn hammer {L. a hammer}. The Latin word used to describe the first bone in our ear, **malleus** with **a hammer**? As I kept the word *hammer* in mind, I quickly moved on to the next bone.

I found that the second bone, incus, has a Latin name also, {L. a anvil). The Latin word used to describe the second bone in our ear is **incus** with an **anvil**? Within our ears, I was led to discover two interesting secrets. But we were not finished yet! As I went on to add the third bone, I discovered an interesting fact that described **the stapes bone**. Its definition was described as the smallest bone of the three with a foot piece that connects to the limb of the incus bone. The stapes bone has a Latin name too; {L. stirrup}.

I was then reminded by my Teacher to visit what is written in Romans 10:17, So then faith *comes* by hearing, and hearing by the word of God.

Then the fuller revelation was made clearer! We must all hear God's word over and over, **like "hammering" on an "anvil"** the word of God **to "stir up" one's faith.**

This design within our ear is undoubtedly the most important of designs to put into action. As representatives of the temple of the Holy Spirit, we have the potential to become unshakeable believers when we begin to stand on and believe for all God's promises. God designed yet another ingenious clever image concerning Him when He designed the bones within the ear. The number *three* is God's image in *divine completeness and perfection.*

Hearing and hearing God's word to stir us up to become unshakeable while standing on all his promises! But there is more!

After we examined the bones in the inner ear, I was led to move on to study how the entire physical ear is divided into three different parts;

1. The external ear,
2. The middle part of the ear,
3. The inner ear.

The outer and external part of the ear is not bone, but is an actual auditory canal between the outer and the middle parts of the human ear. From the outer part of the ear is the place or beginning of where sound waves enter and travels through the ear to be processed.

The **pinna** or **auricle** is the projecting part of the ear that we all can see visually which looks somewhat like a flap.

As sound enters the ear it goes through an auditory canal and strikes the eardrum, as the eardrum vibrates with sound, it moves three small bones, (which will certainly be expounded upon in a minute), which are in the middle ear. These *three bones are called ossicles* and they conduct the sound waves through the stapes. As the stapes moves, it touches a membrane called the oval window which separates the middle ear from the inner ear.

Now as the stapes touches the inner ear with its vibrations it enters into a bony snail-shaped structure called the **cochlea**. Until this study, I never knew that we had a bone in our ear that was shaped like a snail! But the diagram is proof of this design. What was God thinking? Well, inside the *cochlea are three* compartments for the processing of sound that is too complex for even me to explain. There is that number of completion once again, the number three!

Again the incus, malleus, and stapes are the bones of the middle ear. They are the smallest bones in the human body. The three bones are connected by hinges and are levers that carry the vibrations collected from the eardrum to the inner ear.

The mechanical advantage gained in this system increases the volume of the sound *five decibels*, or *about seven times*.

★The number *seven*…God's image in the number *Resurrection; Spiritual completeness; Father's perfection.*

The Table of Showbread and Seven Branched Lamp Stand

The Holy Spirit then directed me to educate myself a little on the significance of the table of showbread and the seven branched lamp stand inside the biblical tabernacle. This was definitely uncharted waters for me, but when I did this is what I discovered; the table of showbread: is representative of the KNOWLEDGE of the Lord Jesus Christ that comes by hearing and hearing the word of God. 2 Peter 3:18 …but grow in grace and knowledge of our Lord and Savior Jesus Christ. To Him *be* the glory both now and forever. Amen.

In the biblical tabernacle the showbread was changed each Sabbath day simply because it was on the Holy and Sanctified day. We are encouraged to study God's Word, fresh and new on a daily basis. FAITH comes by hearing and hearing the word of God through the Gate of our Temple's ear!

It is written in Ezekiel 43:4-6, And the glory of the LORD came into the temple by way of the **gate** which faces toward the east. The spirit lifted me up and brought me into the inner court; and, behold, the glory of the LORD filled the temple. Then I heard *Him* speaking to me from the temple, while a man stood beside me. (emphasis added)

The seven branched lampstand also points to Jesus Christ just as all the other furnishings within the sanctuary. Jesus Himself said, "I am the light of the world. He who follows Me shall not walk in darkness, but have the light of life." (John 8:12)

For it is God who commanded light to shine out of darkness, who has shone in our hearts to *give* **the light of the knowledge of the glory of God** in the face of Jesus Christ. (II Corinthians 4:6) "(emphasis added)"

But what about the oil that is within the lampstand? What does this symbolize? The oil in the lampstand symbolizes the Holy Spirit. The seven branched lampstand represents Jesus as the "light unto the world" if you do not have sufficient "oil" within your vessels, the "light" is diminished and the Christian walk becomes a darkened one. It is "by His Spirit" that we walk and our walk is lighted with His Light? Without the Holy Spirit teaching us the Truth that is in God's Word, the Light would be darkened. Teach me to do Your will, for You are my God; Your Spirit is good. Lead me in the land of uprightness. (Psalm 143:10) However, when He, the Spirit of truth has come, He will guide you into all truth; for He will not speak on His own authority, but whatever He hears He will speak; and He will tell you things to come. (John 16:13)

When the knowledge of the Lord (*the table of showbread*) is heard by the hearing of God's word it then enters the GATE of the ear. "Jesus" this same "WORD", is also represented in the seven branched lamp stand that uses the oil to fuel the light of the Holy Spirit! This is another amazing hidden secret within God's Image!!!

★See the diagram of the inner ear, ear gate that follows this chapter.

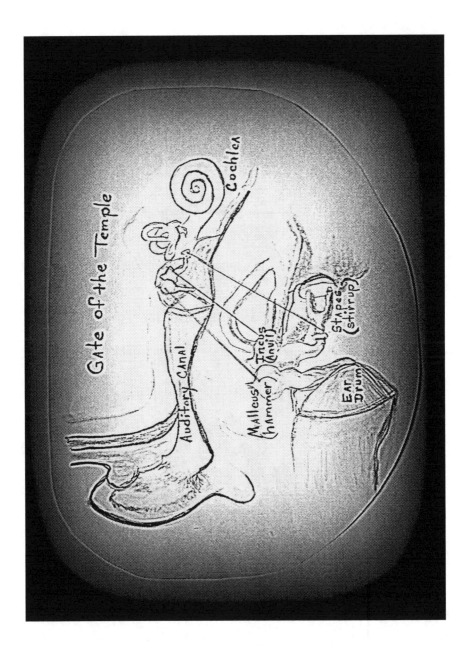

Part 3

Conclusion

Numerical Divine Designs

Chapter 17

Conclusion

Throughout this journey's walk through the temple of our body, it has not been hard to see that the designs through numerical patterns by our Heavenly father have been found to be simply breathtaking. There is no mystery to our God as creator. The *temple* of our body has always had his own little treasure box packed with hidden secrets of God's Image.

Guided by the Holy Spirit, Teacher and Author, each one of God's images were found to support His own specific design according to Genesis 1:26-27!

"Let us make man in our image..." We must not forget that God's first temples were Adam and Eve. They were made specifically for God to have fellowship with them in the garden.

Again, as I said in the introduction of this manuscript, my personal testimony of this walk through the foundation of my body was a gift and I have no reason to believe that it came by no other than the Holy Spirit of our Lord Jesus. It was certainly not in any way meant to be a human anatomy lesson.

Numerical Divine Designs

From the countless numbers of the stars in our solar system down to one of the smallest numerical values in our human body, the only God, the creator of all living creatures great and small;

our Heavenly Father has been, and still is, the greatest designer concerning numerical order from the very beginning of time.

Today in the 21st Century, astrologists through scientology have discovered that there is other complete solar systems way beyond our own. Each neighboring solar system has been duplicated and completed with all nine planets revolving around their own SUN. Each solar system is complete with an array of stars all showing off the magnificent brilliance of God's ongoing handiwork!

★Here is a review of interesting facts within the temple of our body!

Take in consideration first, **the human skull**! Did you know that there are at least **two sets of wings** to be seen that are designed inside of the human skull structure?

1. The greater wings of the sphenoid joins with the outer table of the skull
2. The lesser wings that are on the inner table of the skull

There are also *three layers* of bone around the human skull, and not only that, but there are *three layers* of connective tissue around ones brain with *three* main divisions; the forebrain, the midbrain and the hindbrain.

While we are still on the human skull subject, let's go on and mention that there are *three* parts to each tooth; the crown (the part that projects from the gum), the root (the tooth socket), and thirdly the neck (between root and crown).

On each side of the skull are two ears and in the human ear are 3 bones. Each bone has a symbolic spiritual reason for design.

The number three is repeated through out our human body in various places, so let's take a closer look at the purpose of this numerical value in God's design.

⋆The number three stands for "that which is complete".

We must not forget that God's characteristic is *complete* in the number three; and they are omniscience (all knowing), omnipresent (ever-present) and omnipotence (al-mighty). The very nature of man is made up of three parts: Body, soul and spirit that ultimately makes up mans *complete nature.* God also gives man a *complete gift* packaged in faith, hope and love, and how about the three great divisions of *completing time* of the past, present and future.

In the book of Hosea, one can study our Heavenly Father's numerical design as the prophet Hosea urged the sinning people of the Northern Kingdom to return to the Lord so they could experience salvation *first* through His forgiveness *second;* His healing and *third;* His restoration.

Come, let us return to the LORD; for He has torn, but He will heal us;

He has stricken, but He will bind us up; after two days He will revive us;

on the third day He will rise us up, that we may live in His sight. (Hosea 6:1- 2)

In light of the Old Testament, Hosea also alludes to the *third day* as having been most significant as he reinforced the Lord's healing and restoration was not only certain, but it would be a very special time of victory for God's people.

Jesus taught in Matthew 16:21 that He must be killed and on the *third day* be raised to life. After Jesus' transfiguration, Jesus foretold His disciples in saying, "The Son of Man is about to be betrayed into the hands of men, and they will kill Him, and on the third day He will be raised up." (Matthew 17:22-23)

With the price Jesus paid for us on the cross, there is *total redemption, provision* and *completeness* for all who will receive Him as Savior and Lord. These are free gifts to His children and are the results of Jesus coming to the earth through the virgin birth, dying on the cross then when He rose to life on the third day! All THREE prepared for the bringing to us His total salvation gift through God's divine design.

Here are just a few of other numerical designs of the number three that were found interesting. Our **Hair** has *three* layers: the cuticle, cortex and medulla.

We have *three* basic **Nerve systems:** cranial, spinal and autonomic system. (The autonomic system regulates involuntary organs such as the heart, lungs, intestines, glands, etc.)

We have *three* bones in each **arm:** the humerus, radius and ulna. All three of these bones are designed to work together in completeness.

Our **hands** have *three* groups of bones each: Carpal-wrist, metacarpal-hand and phalanges-digits (fingers).

Our **digits** (fingers) are designed to be *ten* in all.

★The number *ten* is biblically viewed to symbolically represent law, government, and restoration.

Within God's Temple (church) there is only *one* set of Laws: the government rests upon God's shoulders.

★The biblical meaning of the number *one,* is *Unity; New beginnings*

God is the restorer, and the fingers on our hands symbolically represent doing things according to the Kingdom of Heaven for His service.

In Isaiah 9:6 and 7 it is written; For unto us a Child is born, unto us a Son is given: and the government will be upon His shoulder.

And His name will be called Wonderful, Counselor, Mighty God, Everlasting Father, Prince of Peace. Verse7: Of the increase of His government and peace *there will be* no end. Upon the throne of David and over His kingdom, to order it and establish it with judgment and justice from that time forward, even forever. The zeal of the LORD of hosts will perform this.

Our **fingernails and toenails** have *three* parts: the root of the nail, body- where the nail is attached, and bed-under the nail (we only see the bed part when the nail is damaged and comes off).

Our **legs** have *three* bones each: The femur, the largest and strongest: the tibia and the fibula (the tibia is the weight bearing bone or known as the shin bone). All designed to work together!

Our two **feet** have *three* arches each: medial arch, lateral arch and transverse arch. These arches maintain our structural stability. Another interesting note is that there are 7,000 nerves in each foot.

Our **muscles** perform *three functions*, maintaining upright posture, making motion, and generating heat.

There are *three* types of muscles in the body: The skeletal muscle, the smooth muscle and cardiac muscle.

There are *three* major muscles that move the scapula: trapezius muscle, serratus anterior muscle, and the pectoralis minor muscle.

The **trapezius muscle** is very large muscle that drapes over the shoulder and back area in a *triangular* shape with *three* portions. Here again the number *three* meaning complete.

When I first viewed the picture of the back side of the musculoskeletal diagram in my anatomy book, I saw a picture of the many muscles that systematically wrap over each other, (of course this was a view given beneath our skin). But I was particularly drawn to pay closer attention to how the **trapezius muscle** is shaped like a *triangle* in its design. Besides the fact that this muscle was designed to protect the back of the neck muscles, there is a distinct design of the trapezius muscle that also reaches across the back of the skeletal shoulders; side to side and then coming to a point just below the area of the thoracic cavity.

Throughout the entire anatomy study, each *triangular* design had become relevant as the Holy Spirit would allude to completeness as far as any *triangular* shape was concerned. Each triangular design was enlightened upon as been directly in retrospect within God's image as far as representing the Father, the Son and the Holy Spirit, *(the three in one, and commonly known as the trinity of the Godhead.)*

The **sternum has three parts**, the manubrium, the body; and the xiphoid process. Within chapter 9 of the thoracic cavity, Revelations 4:4 has a hidden symbolic design involving the sternum, the sword of the spirit!

The **heart wall** is composed of *three* layers and within the **heart is** *four* chambers, *two* superior atria (interventricualar septum and *two* inferior ventricles).

There are *four* rivers mentioned though out the book of Genesis.

1. The Spirit of the Lord,
2. The river of wisdom and understanding.
3. The river of the spirit of counsel and might.
4. The river of the spirit of knowledge and the fear of the Lord.

I found it most interesting that there is a design that was placed within the heart of man symbolic of these *four* spiritual rivers. These rivers are symbolic within *the four* chambers of the heart circulating the life blood, representative of the life blood of Jesus to keep us not only healthy but spiritually alive. One would have to agree that each river's design is apparently relevant within the heart of the temple of your own body!

The number *five* is found in the human spinal column or vertebral column as it is broken down into *five* regions:

1. The Cervical region (C1–C7)
2. The Thoracic region (TI–T12)
3. The Lumbar region (L1–L5)
4. The Sacral region (S1–5)
5. The fifth region is the Coccyx (tail bone)

★The biblical number *five* symbolically represents *God's grace and God's goodness.*

Within the study of the entire spinal column, the revelation of the hidden design of life and ministry of Jesus our Lord was designed to symbolically represent all of these previous attributes of God's grace and His goodness and so much more.

The number *seven* described in the cervical vertebrae was again symbolically revealed by the Holy Spirit as meaning Resurrection, Spiritual completeness and the Father's perfection

It was a privilege and an honor to have taken this walk through the Temple with the understanding of the Holy Spirit.

God Himself through His Holy Spirit has revealed His images in a most intimate and miraculous way through our bone placements.

The mystery behind the boney smile on the human skull's expression was never meant to be used for evil, it was designed in God's own way for expressing the wording in Genesis 1:31, *And God saw everything that he had made, and, behold, it was very good!*

Biblical Numbers	Meanings
1	Unity; New beginnings
2	Union; Division; Witnessing
3	Divine completeness and perfection
4	Creation; The world; Creative works
5	Grace; God's goodness
6	Weakness of man; Manifestation of sin; Evils of Satan
7	Resurrection; Spiritual completeness; Father's perfection
8	New Birth; New Beginnings
9	Fruit of the spirit; Divine completeness from the Father
10	Testimony; Law and responsibility
11	Disorder and judgment
12	Governmental perfection
13	Apostasy; depravity and rebellion
14	Deliverance; Salvation
15	Rest
16	Love
17	Victory
18	Bondage
19	Faith
20	Redemption
21	Exceeding sinfulness of sin
22	Light
23	Death
24	The Priesthood
25	Repentance; The forgiveness of sins
26	The Gospel of Christ
27	Preaching of the Gospel
28	Eternal life
29	Departure
30	Blood of Christ; Dedication

Biblical Numbers	Meanings
31	Offspring
32	Covenant
33	Promise
34	Naming of a Son
35	Hope
36	Enemy
37	The word of our Father
38	Slavery
39	Disease
40	Trials; Probation; Testings
42	Israel's oppression; First advent
44	Judgment of the World
45	Preservation
50	Holy Spirit; Pentecost
60	Pride
66	Idol worship
70	Punishment and restoration of Israel; Universality
100	Election; Children of promise
119	Spiritual perfection and victory $7 \star 17 = 119$
120	Divine period of probation
144	The Spirit guided life
200	Insufficiency
600	Warfare
666	Antichrist
777	Christ
888	Holy Spirit; The sum of Tree of Life
1000	Divine completeness and Father's glory
4000	Salvation of the world through the blood of the Lamb (Those who choose between Christ and Antichrist)
6000	Deception of Antichrist; Second Advent
7000	Final judgment; Zadok
144,000	Those numbered of Israel

I have to admit, I am guilty of picking up a book and flipping to the last page to see how a book ends. I even find comfort in reading the last page of the Holy Bible; as I can find myself discouraged at times to the events that are taking shape in the world around me. It is written that, The Lord God wins over all in the end. I find so much comfort in knowing that. He is coming for all people who have kept His word Holy and not distorted them.

So, even though you might start out a little skeptical about this book at first, I believe when you go back to the front and walk through the temple of your own body, you can walk away with positive edification for living for Jesus Christ. This book contains eye-opening information that is non-denominational and is for all people, worldwide. You will understand just how our bodies are fearfully and wonderfully made and why the Holy Spirit of God has gone the extra mile to tell us WHY He loves us.

This is a definite call for the nations to return to the one and true God: The same God that made Adam and Eve: The same God of and all the descendents of Abraham, Isaac, and Jacob. God said, … "If my people who are called by My name will humble themselves, and pray and seek My face, and turn from their wicked ways, then I will hear from heaven, and will forgive their sin and heal their land." (II Chronicles 7:14) We need desperate healing in our land!

With a grateful heart, I clearly recognize the Holy Spirit as the true Author and Teacher behind my testimony.

Terry Jane Swiger 2014

References materials

1. The hidden secrets of God's image were revealed to me by the Holy Spirit.
2. New Spirit Filled Life Bible, Thomas Nelson Bible…says:

   Any use of the NKJV text must include a proper acknowledgment as follows: Scripture taken from the New King James Version. Copyright @1982 by Thomas Nelson, Inc.

3. Stedman's Concise Medical & Allied Health Dictionary:

   Illustrated. 3rd edition. Copyright @ 1997 Williams & Wilkins

4. Edition 25, Dorland's Pocket Medical Dictionary, WB. Saunders Company
5. Biblical Numbers Quick Reference: This is the chart that I included in Part of my manuscript as a reference for the readers.

   www.spiritcommunity.com (I'm not sure about this web site. I had to type in Biblical Numbers Quick Reference to get to the chart.)

6. At Home Professions:

   Anatomy and Physiology (for Medical Transcriptionists)
   A Terminology-In-Action Textbook

7. Used No Quotes from but studied: Human Anatomy & Physiology, Forth Edition by Elaine N. Marieb.
8. A paraphrased quote from the late Oral Roberts on Faith.
9. The photo images belong to the author.